The Dalesman Guide to the North York Moors

Lealholmside, Eskdale (*Elizabeth Gray*)

The Dalesman Guide to the

North York Moors

DALESMAN BOOKS
1982

The Dalesman Publishing Company Ltd.,
Clapham, via Lancaster, LA2 8EB.

First published 1982

ISBN: 0 85206 665 1

Printed by Galava Printing Company Limited, Nelson, Lancashire

Contents

Cover photograph of Goathland by C. R. Kilvington.

Map on page 6 courtesy North York Moors National Park.
Text on pages 10 - 13 courtesy Forestry Commission.

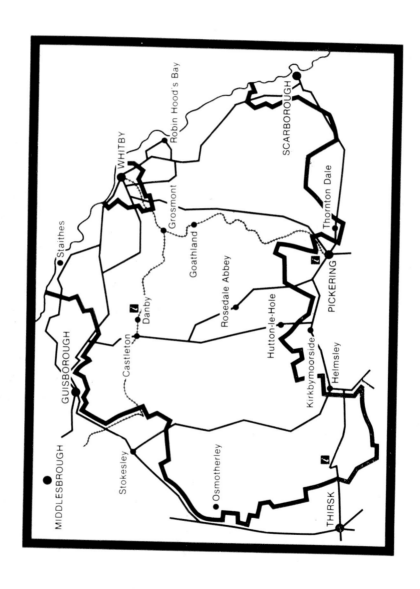

6

Introduction

THE North York Moors cover some 553 square miles which together form an isolated region of moorland and dales, rising above adjacent lowland plains. This fine expanse of open countryside was officially designated as a National Park in 1952—a move to ensure the preservation of its natural beauty.

The towns of Guisborough, Whitby, Scarborough and Thirsk mark the extreme corners of the North York Moors. Easily defined by physical boundaries—that is, the Vale of Pickering (south), the Vales of York and Mowbray (west), the flat levels of the Cleveland Plain and Teesside (north) and the 25 miles of North Sea coastline (east)—the moorlands maintain elements of an unchanged rural England with remote hamlets and villages aside rivers and vales.

Characteristic of the area is the moorland heather. This smothers the tops in great abundance providing textural contrast with the intermittent dales. While heather survives on the moorland acid soils, the softer valleys support a variety of forestry plantations and rich farmland. Eighty per cent of the National Park falls under private ownership. Careful management policies result in a fertile and productive land.

The pattern of extensive moorland and narrow dales is broken in the west by ranges of highland—the Cleveland Hills and the Hambletons, and in the east by a variety of rugged coastline reaching from Scarborough to as far north as Staithes. This diversity of scenery within such a compact area proves an attraction to any visitor!

The Hambleton Hills run south from Osmotherley down to Sutton Bank and around to Helmsley at a height of up to 1,000 feet. On this steep western escarpment, above the village of Kilburn, lies the well-known landmark—the limestone 'White Horse'. The Tabular Hills, also of limestone, stand between Helmsley and Scarborough—a flat plateau some two to three miles wide, where the land rises from the Vale of Pickering.

The heather-topped Cleveland Hills extend north-east from Osmotherley forming the northern profile of the moors. The highest point within the region (1,489ft) is at Botton Head on Urra Moor. The hills show evidence of the area's industrial past with remnants of jet, alum and ironstone mines among the wildness of the moorland landscape.

Limestone and sandstone are the most dominant rocks in the North York Moors, indicated largely by boundary walls which graduate from shades of

7

grey to brown. The central moors around Westerdale and Wheeldale are of sandstone. The curious honey-coloured stone as seen in settlements such as Pickering and Helmsley is often referred to as sandy-limestone—it is in fact limestone with a large proportion of sand and iron.

Features of historical interest are prevalent throughout the National Park. In addition to traces of an active industrial past, historic monuments survive from as early as 3000 B.C. Burial grounds from the New Stone Age (3000 - 1800 B.C.) and several tumuli and howes of the Bronze Age (1800 - 500 B.C.) are found across the moors. On Wheeldale Moor, some 600 feet above sea level, are 1¼ miles of preserved Roman road. Of greater significance are the castles and abbeys, which collectively date back over 800 years. Ancient fortifications remain at Helmsley, Pickering and Scarborough, together with the atmospheric ruins of abbeys such as Rievaulx and Byland. Rievaulx in particular pays tribute to the success of the monastic period, the foundation stone of this Cistercian community being laid in 1131.

The North Yorkshire Moors Railway and the museums at Pickering and Hutton-le-Hole offer local history of a slightly different nature. While steam trains wind their way through otherwise inaccessible Newtondale, the Ryedale Folk Museum at Hutton-le-Hole recaptures much of the area's industrial and cultural past. By contrast, present day attractions include a variety of settlements and thriving market towns, as well as peaceful valleys such as Rosedale and Farndale.

In all, the North York Moors has a considerable potential for the walker as well as the motorist. Ideally situated in the north-east of England, the region remains relatively undiscovered by modern standards of tourism. There are over a thousand miles of public footpaths and bridleways within the National Park, in addition to outstanding stretches of road which reach over the moors' exposed heights.

This book forms a basic guide for the visitor to the North York Moors National Park. In addition to sections on the forests, the North Yorkshire Moors Railway, recommended walks and drives, it covers the region in six areas, the outstanding features of which are described in narrative form on pages 15 to 44. Practical information on the same areas is contained in the Reference Section on pages 69 - 95, which summarises the facilities of the main centres, opening times of places to visit, nature trails, information centres, youth hostels, caravan sites, fishing and riding.

The arrangement of the areas begins with the south-east, the first part of the North York Moors to be seen by visitors en route to Scarborough or Whitby via Thirsk. 'Helmsley and the Hambletons' takes in the whole of Bilsdale as well as the southern edge of the escarpment around Kilburn, Coxwold and Ampleforth. Moving east, 'Kirkbymoorside and the Southern Dales' includes the valleys of Bransdale, Farndale and Rosedale, while 'Pickering and the South-East' embraces Newtondale as well as the extensive Dalby Forest. 'The Esk Valley' describes the dale and its many tributaries—an area stretching from Commondale to Sleights. Finally, the north-western fringe from Osmotherley to Guisborough is covered in

'Cleveland Hills and Plain', while 'Whitby and the Coast' focuses on such settlements as Staithes, Runswick and Robin Hood's Bay.

Lilla Cross, near Goathland (*J. C. Longstaff*)

The Forests of
the North York Moors

THERE are 60,000 acres (23,000 hectares) of Forestry Commission land within the North York Moors National Park. In contrast to much of the Park, this is land in public ownership and visitors are welcome to walk as they please in any area identified by the distinctive Forestry Commission signboard. Planting began in the 1920s and felling of the oldest trees began in the 1970s. Now over 70,000 tonnes of timber leave the forests every year, the bulk of it to be used as saw timber or as pitwood for the mines of South Yorkshire and the Midlands. Forestry is one of the area's major employers, with over 300 people involved in felling trees, planting and managing the forest, and maintaining buildings, car parks and forest walks.

The forest rewards patience and attention to detail. It is not as immediately attractive or exciting as some of the area's landscapes. But spend a little time and discover dramatic views, hidden streams and clearings, and an unexpected wealth of wildlife that gradually reveals itself to the careful observer. To find the most attractive places visit the forest drives, car parks, picnic places and forest walks which are scattered throughout the North York Moors forests. Or perhaps, stay in Cropton Forest at Spiers House Campsite or at Keldy Castle Forest Cabins.

The largest forests are concentrated in the south-east of the National Park, between Pickering, Scarborough and Whitby. Most popular, and as suitable for a short visit as a full day out, is the **Dalby Forest Drive**. Approaching Low Dalby village from Thornton Dale, the road dips away and the valley comes into view between the trees. Stop for a moment in the layby. Dalby has an Information Centre, featuring a diorama of forest wildlife and selling a wide range of leaflets and other publications.

A short walk down to the beck is worthwhile. In spring, listen for the siskin's song flight. This small green and yellow finch is a recent addition to North Yorkshire's breeding birds, attracted by the maturing conifer forests. Its nest is the hardest to find of any British bird, 60 or 80 feet up a mature conifer, and then balanced out at the tip of a branchlet. As the singing male flies over, a "window" in its wing can be seen against the light, an almost transparent bar of yellow feathers. Both pied and grey wagtail nest during summer and dipper can often be seen from the bridge at any time of year. Keep an eye out for a kingfisher.

Scattered along the nine mile forest drive are many parking places, picnic sites and waymarked forest walks. A leaflet is available for the **Sneverdale Forest Walk**, which starts half a mile north of Low Dalby, giving information on the forest operations, trees, animals and plants to be seen along it.

Three miles further is Staindale. Walk from here to the National Trust's Bridestones or to the Staindale Lake. The car park at the far end of the lake has a special unloading bay and path to allow wheelchair access to the water's edge, and the Staindale toilet block also has facilities for the disabled. In winter, take some bread to feed the mallard. Little grebe breed most years, but are very secretive when there are many people about. Birdwatchers come to Dalby specially to see another coniferous forest finch, the crossbill. Named for its remarkable bill, adapted specifically for extracting conifer seed from the cone, it can be seen anywhere in Dalby, including Dalby village, though in some years crossbills are rather elusive. The male is a bright scarlet bird, the size of a bullfinch.

A steep hill leads onto Allerston Low Moor, a flat area of poor soils which have a thin, hard "iron pan", preventing deep rooting and resulting in slow tree growth. Felled and replanted areas have been ploughed to a depth of one metre to break this pan. A spur road leads to Crosscliffe car park. Walk the 200 yard path, between the prehistoric Dargate Dykes, to a superb view over the Crossville valley, the young forest of the Allerston and Wykeham High Moors to the white spheres of Fylingdales Early Warning Station.

The **Falling Foss Forest Walk** is a pleasant day out from Whitby. The car parks at Maybecks and Falling Foss are linked by a circular, waymarked walk for which a leaflet (10p) is available. Maybecks, with grassy slopes clipped short by sheep and a shallow rocky stream, is a particularly pleasant spot for a picnic. The Falling Foss itself is a dramatic waterfall, set in one of the finest broadleaved woodland valleys of the National Park. But as the valley, and the forest walk, climb towards the moors, oak and beech give way to scrub birch and finally the coniferous plantations of Sneaton High Moor. The leaflet charts this succession, naming many of the trees and plants characteristic of each habitat type.

For visitors on foot the North Yorkshire Moors Railway provides access to the heart of an area of outstanding scenery and forest. Alight from the train at **Newtondale Halt** into a natural cathedral of towering cliffs enframed by mature spruce. Three waymarked walks lead through the forest. The easiest is a gentle stroll along the valley bottom to Rapers Farm picnic site. The Needle Point and Levisham Station walks involve a steep climb, rewarded by dramatic views over the 200 foot deep valley. This valley is as good a place as any to see one of the area's numerous but elusive roe deer, which have become common as the forests have developed. It is also a stronghold of the nocturnal badger, thriving in setts winding into crevices in the rock of the valley side. Again, a leaflet (20p) is available describing in more detail the geology, history and wildlife of this remote and fascinating place.

To the west, leading either from the National Park's Sutton Bank car park or from the White Horse car park, is the **White Horse Walk**. Although the famous Kilburn White Horse is its principle feature, this walk also gives exceptional views over the Vale of York to the Yorkshire Dales.

The 15 mile **Reasty to Allerston Walk** (Allerston is on the main A170

The extensively forested glacial gorge of Newtondale. Several waymarked walks lead through the forest from Newtondale Halt on the North Yorkshire Moors Railway. (*Alec Wright*)

east of Pickering) is an exception to the usual moderate length, circular walks described above, and it is necessary to arrange to be picked up at the far end, or check bus times. Designed for the serious walker, it provides an unparalleled experience of the North Yorkshire forests. Leaflets are available (both 5p each) for these walks.

For the camper and caravanner, Spiers House campsite just north of Pickering is set in the 10,000 acre **Cropton Forest**. It has a full range of facilities, including toilets and showers. It is open from early April until the end of September, and is run on a first come first served basis. Keldy Castle Forest Cabins, also in Cropton Forest, have 60 luxury Scandinavian style self catering cabins. The site has extensive facilities, for the use of residents exclusively, including several waymarked forest walks, a nature trail, pony trekking, badminton, squash, table tennis, a cafe and a coin-op laundry. Booking is essential and for further information on both Keldy and Spiers please write to Forest Holidays, Forestry Commission, 231 Corstorphine Road, Edinburgh, EH12 7AT. Although both sites are excellently situated for touring the National Park, it is the forest which

12

attracts many visitors. Deer, sparrowhawk, adder and woodcock are just a selection of the wildlife to be seen and a specially designed hide for the use of Keldy residents has given many children their first exciting view of a badger. Cropton is one of the strongholds of the increasingly rare, nocturnal nightjar, whose peculiar churring song can be heard from the cabins during June and July, and tawny owls regularly nest in specially provided boxes.

Newgate Bank, Cowhouse Bank and **Clay Bank** are all forest car parks with excellent views. There are many other forest car parks and picnic places scattered throughout the National Park. Forest walks in **Wykeham Forest**, just north Wykeham village near Scarborough, lead through one of the country's largest forest nurseries. The specialist naturalist can obtain information from the Yorkshire Naturalist's Trust on the nature reserves it leases within the forest.

Please enjoy your forests, their peace, scenery and wildlife, while you are on holiday in the North York Moors National Park. Just one request: do not light fires of any sort in the forest and if you do spot a forest fire please dial 999 and report it to the Fire Brigade.

For further information write to the Forestry Commission, Pickering District Office, 42 Eastgate, Pickering, North Yorkshire, YO18 7DU. Please add postage to orders for leaflets.

Sutton Bank, looking towards the gliding station. (*Bernard Fearnley*)

Helmsley and
the Hambletons

AN attractive market town on the edge of the moors, **Helmsley** is also an excellent tourist centre and a place of great history encompassed by a wealth of ancient monuments. Its outstanding feature is the dignified market place, dominated by the half-timbered Black Swan and surrounded by other inns and cafes which make the town such a popular stopping place for travellers en route from West Yorkshire to the coast. The square contains a market cross and a large obelisk—a memorial to the second Baron Feversham. Nearby is All Saints Church, an imposing building heavily restored in 1866 but still containing a Norman chancel arch and another Norman arch over the south door. A Norse hogsback stone is to be seen in the church porch.

Opposite the church is the path to Helmsley Castle, the ruined keep of which dominates the town. Of ancient origin, the earliest parts of the building date from about 1200 when Robert de Roos was Lord of Helmsley. Slighted in the civil war in 1644, its chief interest today is the elaborate system of earthworks including double defensive ditches of great size. Apart from the keep, other surviving portions of note include the barbican, the west tower and the domestic outbuildings within which are some 16th century plaster friezes.

A later Lord of Helmsley created the fine mansion of Duncombe Park, employing the architect William Wakefield who was probably advised by John Vanbrugh. Now a girls' school, it stands clear of the town among a landscape of woodland and plains, temples and terraces which provide a delightful prospect of the river Rye.

The terrace is repeated to even better effect at **Rievaulx**, two miles north-west of Helmsley just off the main Bilsdale road. A great stretch of greensward nearly half a mile long has a temple at each end, one in Ionic style and the other of the Tuscan order. At intervals along the Terrace (now in the care of the National Trust), vistas have been cut through the wooded hillside to give magnificent views of Rievaulx Abbey below. Like most Cistercian foundations, the abbey itself is tucked away from the sight of the world and is reached with a sense of discovery. It was in fact a prototype in Yorkshire, being the first abbey connected with the order to be established in the county. Walter Espec, Lord of Helmsley, was the man who made it possible in 1131. There was little suitable terrain here for a large church and so it was set almost due north and south, going against general custom. The ruined nave, with its nine bays, impresses even today because it is 170 feet long. The effect over 800 years ago, when buildings were normally very small, can be imagined.

Rievaulx Abbey can be reached either from Helmsley or from Sutton Bank via **Scawton**, a small village with a church and an inn that once claimed to be the smallest in Yorkshire. The church has a remarkable interior featuring a Norman chancel arch, recesses with squints and a piscina. The bell is from Byland Abbey and is one of the oldest in England. Bells once caused a great problem at nearby **Old Byland**, where a monastery was founded by monks from Furness Abbey in 1143. It proved to be too close to the Cistercian foundation at Rievaulx—each monastery could hear the bells of the other by day and night, 'which was not fitting and could by no means be endured'. Eventually the newcomers gave way and moved to establish the abbey at Byland.

The road northwards from Helmsley to Stokesley runs through the fine valley scenery of **Bilsdale**, dotted with isolated farms. Just over three miles from Helmsley a left fork leads to **Hawnby**, a lovely village dominated by the twin limestone nabs of Easterside and Hawnby Hill. Delightful upland roads lead across the moors to Boltby via Sneck Yate Bank and to Osmotherley—the latter has an attractive parking and picnic spot at Ellers Wood.

The main road up Bilsdale climbs to the top of **Newgate Bank**, from where there is a good view along the length of the valley to the Cleveland Hills beyond. Two miles beyond the foot of the bank is the Sun Inn, better known as Spout House, with its recently restored cruck building—the original inn. At the head of the dale is **Chop Gate**, locally pronounced 'Chop Yat', beyond which the main road climbs to Clay Bank and a side road diverges to Carlton Bank (see 'Cleveland Hills and Plain').

Bilsdale is good walking country, a particularly fine route extending along Roppa Edge from the Newgate Bank car park and offering extensive views as it climbs above the 1,000 ft. contour. It curves round to the western side of Riccal Dale and after about two miles comes to some distinctive aluminium sculptures commissioned by the Yorkshire Arts Association from Mr Austin Wright. They have not been universally acclaimed. The sculptures can also be reached by a four mile gated road which begins near Helmsley church.

Many visitors to Helmsley and the North York Moors reach the area from Thirsk along the A170, one of the most spectacular lengths of main road in England. In a little over half a mile it climbs more than 500 feet, by means of 1 in 4 gradients and acute bends, to the top of **Sutton Bank**. Here, on the north side of the road, are two large car parks and a tourist information centre with snack bar and toilets. It is a compelling place to stop, especially on a clear day when the panorama extends to York, Knaresborough, Richmond and the high peaks of the Pennines. There is a direction indicator on the south side of the road, beyond which a walk along the cliff top leads to the White Horse of Kilburn (see below). On the breezy plateau are the headquarters of the Yorkshire Gliding Club—

16

The rolling valley landscape of the North York Moors as seen in the upper reaches of Ryedale. In the middle distance is Hawnby, sheltered from the north by its distinctive limestone nab. (*Clifford Robinson*)

if the weather conditions are satisfactory, one can watch gliders wheeling in the air and landing on the grass runway just yards from the path. Brooding below the escarpment is the mysterious-looking Lake Gormire which has neither feeder nor outlet and was once reputed to be bottomless.

The low-level route from Thirsk to Helmsley passes through the Gilling Gap, separating the Hambletons from the Howardian Hills and containing several noteworthy villages. **Kilburn,** with a stream running alongside its main street, is famous as the home of Robert Thompson, the woodcarver who used the mouse as his trademark on all his furniture. His workshops and showrooms in the centre of the village are almost surrounded by stacks of oak planks seasoning. The work of Thompson is to be seen in churches throughout the country; fuller details are given in the Dalesman book 'The Mouseman of Kilburn' by James Thompson.

North of the village on Roulston Scar is the **White Horse of Kilburn,** reached by a twisting and steep road locally known as 'the mare's tail'.

17

The soaring arches of Rievaulx Abbey. (*S. Preston*)

There is a car park sufficient for 100 vehicles near the legs of the beast. The horse was commissioned by Thomas Taylor, a native of Kilburn who made a fortune in London as a merchant, and was carved by John Hodgson, the local schoolmaster, and 32 villagers between October 28th and November 4th, 1857. Measuring 314 feet by 228 feet it has to be periodically restored and dressed with chalk brought from the Yorkshire Wolds.

Two miles south of Kilburn is **Coxwold**, a picture-postcard village which attracts many visitors. Its broad, sloping street is bordered by neat grass verges and mellow stone cottages. The crowning glory is the octagonal tower of the parish church, an ornate perpendicular building with an aisle-less interior, a three-decker pulpit and much stained glass. The best-known incumbent was Laurence Sterne, who while residing here from 1760 to 1768 completed 'Tristram Shandy' and wrote 'The Sentimental Journey' and 'Journal to Eliza'. A noted wit as well as a novelist, his home was nearby Shandy Hall, a fascinating brick house with an enormous stone chimney. It is now open to the public.

The road leading south from Coxwold soon passes **Newburgh Priory**, established by Augustinian canons in 1145. After the dissolution it was turned into a splendid country house, set in a park with a lake, and was later occupied by one Baron Fauconburg who married Mary, the daughter of Oliver Cromwell. A tradition holds that she had Cromwell's body removed from Westminster Abbey to the Priory where it was placed in a secret vault, and that when the restoration occurred it was a substitute body which was exhumed and hung at Tyburn.

Only two miles to the north in this area which found such favour in monastic times is **Byland Abbey**, founded in 1177 after the vicissitudes noted above. It is not as complete as Rievaulx but much of the west end remains including the lower part of the rose window. The largest Cistercian church in England, it measured 330 feet long by 140 feet wide and was paved with green and yellow glazed tiles in geometrical patterns—examples in an almost perfect state of preservation can be seen in the two chapels in the south transept. A short distance along the road to Oldstead is the abbey gate house.

East of Byland, the road hugs the southern edge of the Hambleton Hills, passing through the small village of **Wass** where many of the houses are probably built of stone from the abbey. A steep and long climb up Wass Bank leads to the main Thirsk - Helmsley road. **Ampleforth** is notable not so much for the village itself, which consists of one long street nearly half a mile long, but for its great Benedictine abbey and school situated nearly a mile to the east. The abbey was founded in 1802 as St Laurence's Priory by a community of English Benedictines, who from the outset ran a school which has steadily increased in size and prestige. Dominant among the many fine buildings is the abbey church, begun in 1924 to the designs of Sir Gilbert Scott and not completed until over 30 years later.

In 1929 the school acquired **Gilling Castle** as its preparatory college. It stands just outside the village of Gilling East (so named to distinguish it

Cherry blossom, mellow stone, red pantiles and church tower combine to form a delightful scene at Kirkbymoorside. (*A. W. Curtis*)

from its namesake near Richmond) on the Helmsley - York road. The present castle, although having a 14th century basement, dates largely from Elizabethan times. The work of Sir William Fairfax, its glory is the great dining room—at one stage all the decorations were sold to an American but these were later recovered and the room restored!

Kirkbymoorside and the Southern Dales

KIRKBYMOORSIDE is missed by many travellers en route from Helmsley to Pickering and the coast—which is a pity. Bypassed by the main road, it is a place of considerable character on less formal lines than Helmsley. The cobbled market place is dominated by the toll booth—built of stone from a former castle—and boasts a distinctive market cross. It is surrounded by an abundance of old inns: the White Horse which once had its own pew in the parish church, the Black Swan with a timber-framed porch dated 1634, and among others the King's Head with its Buckingham Room, a reminder of the 2nd Duke of Buckingham who died in the house next door. John Gibson rode over from the mansion at Welburn Hall to settle the Duke's affairs but found not a penny left—he had spent a fortune, lived like a king and died a pauper!

Also bypassed a little more than a mile to the west towards Helmsley is **St Gregory's Minster, Kirkdale.** Reached by a side road which goes through a water splash, it is an enchanting place whose history goes back over 1,300 years. A small building—and not as some imagine a massive cathedral church—its nave was built prior to the Norman Conquest and contains two magnificent Saxon stone coffin lids under the arcade of the north aisle. Its outstanding feature is the dial stone inside the porch over the south door. The finest remaining example of an Anglo-Saxon sundial, it shows how the Angles divided the hours of daylight into 'tides' and also records the rebuilding of the church between 1050 and 1065. Written in Northumbrian English with occasional runic letters, the inscription states: 'Orm Gamal's Son bought St Gregory's Minster when it was all broken down and fallen in and he let it be made anew from the ground to Christ and St Gregory, in Edward's days, the King, and in Tosti's days, the Earl.' Close to the ford is Kirkdale Cave where in 1821 were found the remains of 300 hyenas as well as the bones of many other animals including bear, tiger, elephant, bison, reindeer, deer and wolf. At the time the discovery was held up as proof that Noah's flood had affected Yorkshire!

Hodge Beck which flows through Kirkdale has its headwaters in **Bransdale**, a remote valley with a wild charm all of its own which can be reached from Helmsley by way of Carlton, Riccal Dale and East Moors. The route passes the quaint moorland church of St Mary Magdalene, East Moors, minute in size and designed by Temple Moor in 1882. Bransdale can also be approached from Kirkbymoorside via Fadmoor or

Gillamoor, noted for its 'surprise view' as one rounds the corner near the church.

The view extends up **Farndale,** one of the best known valleys in Yorkshire as a result of its famous daffodils. These are concentrated in the lower and middle portions of the dale and are best seen from the 1½ mile walk beside the river Dove from Low Mill to Church Houses. According to local lore they were originally planted by the monks. Many visitors make the mistake of timing their daffodil safari before the blooms are at their best; the inhabitants of Farndale claim that the third and fourth week in April is the most rewarding time to see the feast of yellow fragrance. A one-way traffic system is in operation during this period to prevent disaster on the narrow lanes. It must be stressed that one should stand and stare but not pick the flowers, which are now protected by law.

The road encircling Farndale from Gillamoor leads at the other side of the valley to **Hutton-le-Hole,** one of the show villages of Yorkshire. With red-tiled buildings looking at each other across tracts of verdant grass, and becks crossed by white-painted footbridges, this is a most unusual village. Grass soon gives way to heather and the moors are seen stretching to distant horizons. Undoubtedly the main tourist attraction is the Ryedale Folk Museum, begun by the late R.W. Crosland and continued with unabated enthusiasm by Bertram Frank, a local farmer. This living museum now has over 20,000 exhibits and more than 50,000 visitors per year. There are annual festivities on the first Saturday in May when it is possible to watch a woman in old-time dress spinning wool, a blacksmith at work at a forge that has been brought here with all its accessories and children dancing round a maypole. Other buildings that have been shifted here—often stone by stone, timber by timber, tile by tile—have included a cruck farmhouse from Danby, a glass furnace from Rosedale, a manor house and a cottage from Harome and a splendid 19th century horse wheel and shed. A walk round the museum will give a lot of information to anyone exploring the North York Moors.

Little more than a mile due east is another of the glories of Yorkshire in the ancient and inspiring church at **Lastingham.** A monastery was built here in 654 A.D. but destroyed by the Danes some 200 years later. Then in 1078 a community of Benedictine monks from Whitby settled on the same site and began building a great church; however, with only the east end complete, they moved to York and founded St Mary's Abbey. The works at Lastingham were finished off with west wall, buttresses and tower to form a village church that has more the spaciousness of a cathedral. Beneath it is a crypt, built by the monks almost a thousand years ago, which is a little church in itself, complete with sanctuary, nave and aisles, with a stone-vaulted roof supported by Norman piers and capitals. Objects of interest on display include a collection of ancient stones and the horizontal portion of an enormous cross.

South of Lastingham are the picturesque villages of **Appleton-le-Moors,** with its wide main street, and **Sinnington,** where the river Seven flows past the tall maypole surmounted by a fox—a reminder that this is classic

St. Gregory's Minster, Kirkdale, is famed for the Saxon sundial in its porch. (*P. Rennison*)

fox-hunting country. A third settlement close to the river is **Cropton,** birthplace of William Scoresby, the Arctic whaling captain.

The Seven rises in **Rosedale,** a harsher valley than Farndale with its steep slopes virtually denuded of trees. The main settlement is Rosedale Abbey, named after a Cistercian nunnery founded in 1190—the present-day church stands on the site of the original chapel. From here a road heads north-east over the moors to Egton Bridge in Eskdale. In the opposite direction one of the steepest roads in England reaches Hutton-le-Hole after surmounting the 1 in 3 bank known as Rosedale Chimney. The name derives from the chimney which until 1972 stood close to the top of the hill and formed part of the former Rosedale West ironstone mines. Prior to closure in 1929 these were served by a remarkable railway which ran along the edge of the valley and around the head of Farndale, reaching a summit level of over 1,300 feet before descending abruptly to Battersby by means of a rope-worked incline. A branch passed round the head of

Rosedale from Blakey Junction to calcining kilns on the east side of the valley. Much of the route today remains easy to follow—and indeed a substantial stretch forms part of the Lyke Wake Walk.

Hutton-le-Hole, with its beck, spacious green and thriving folk museum, is one of the most visited places in the North York Moors. (*Clifford Robinson*)

Pickering and
the South-East

OCCUPYING a key position at the intersection of the main roads from Thirsk to Scarborough and Malton to Whitby, **Pickering** is an ancient place which reputedly derived its name in a remarkable way. According to tradition it was founded in 270 B.C. by King Peredurus who lost a ring in the nearby river Costa and accused a maid of the household of its theft. A cook in the royal kitchen later found the ring, swallowed from the river by a pike, as he prepared it for the table. In remorse the king married the lady—and bestowed the name Pike-ring on the settlement to commemorate his betrothment.

The main roads miss the most interesting part of the town which has at its centre the Market Place rising towards the church. Shops and houses back on to the small churchyard giving little indication that here is one of the most fascinating churches in the north of England. Its transepts and chantry chapel, carved monuments of local knights and great porch reflect the prosperity of Pickering and its woolmen in medieval times. Its proudest feature is the unique set of early 15th century frescoes which adorn both sides of the nave. For many years hidden under numerous coats of whitewash, they were re-discovered in 1853 and have progressively been restored. Among the scenes depicted are St George slaying the dragon, Herod's Feast, the martyrdom of Thomas a Becket, the story of St Catherine of Alexandria and the seven corporal Acts of Mercy.

Close to the church are Willowgate and Boroughgate, leading into Castlegate where stands a royal fortification. **Pickering Castle** began as a motte and bailey in the late 11th century, the earth mound offering a fine view of the surrounding district. Within the bailey are the foundations of the old hall, with the royal seat still visible where King John once lost ten shillings playing backgammon with the Earl of Salisbury. Richard II was imprisoned in the doorless tower next to the keep, whilst other towers were named after the Fair Rosamund and the Devil himself. The remains of the new hall, built by Earl Thomas of Lancaster survive close to the chantry chapel. The castle reached its peak in the early part of the 14th century with the construction of the outer curtain wall and thereafter declined; it was taken by Cromwell's forces in the Civil War but returned to the Duchy of Lancaster on the restoration of the monarchy. It is now in the care of the Department of the Environment.

A right turn on leaving the castle leads steeply downhill to the Under-

Above: Sugar Loaf Hill, Low Langdale, close to the Hackness end of the Forest Drive. (*Alec Wright*)
Opposite: Smiddy Hill, Pickering, with the parish church in the background.
(*J. J. Thomlinson*)

cliffe, where to the left is Pickering station, headquarters of the North Yorkshire Moors Railway (see separate chapter). To the right, on the road to Newbridge, are **Moorland Trout Farms** where rainbow trout are reared in large square ponds containing between 15,000 and 50,000 fish ranging in size from an inch to two feet long. Fish for the freezer or more instant consumption can be bought at a shop which is open daily.

At the south end of the Undercliffe a right turn leads into Bridge Street, on the right of which is the **Beck Isle Museum of Rural Life**. It contains a collection of items from the 19th and early 20th centuries displayed in appropriate settings, such as a gents outfitters, an ironmongers, a cobblers, a village shop and a Victorian pub. There are also wheelwright's and cooper's workshops, a saddlery and a printing shop.

From Bridge Street a walk along Train Lane or Potter Hill leads to the main Thirsk-Scarborough road which crosses Pickering Beck and enters the centre of the town along Hungate. Here is Houndgate Hall, former home of Dr. John Kirk who created the Kirk collection which became the nucleus of York Castle Museum. In recent times it became James Herriot's 'Skeldale House' during the filming of 'All Creatures Great and Small'; the Hall is not open to the public.

A little over three miles south of Pickering off the Malton road is **Kirby Misperton,** home of the Flamingoland leisure complex. It boasts a zoo with numerous animals, birds and reptiles, a dolphinarium, a fairground, 'cowboy city', boating lake and picnic site. In complete contrast in the opposite direction is **Newton-on-Rawcliffe**, reached from Pickering along the Undercliffe road past the station. It stands on a hill top above

26

Newtondale and offers a fine view of the gorge from a side road at the top of the village. The road to Cropton passes Elleron View, where there is a panorama over the vast Cropton Forest, and also Cawthorn Camp— probably built by the Romans about 110 A.D.—which can be reached along a signposted track.

The main road to Whitby climbs steadily out of Pickering and gives some tantalising glimpses of Newtondale before striding purposefully across the moors. After five miles a left turn leads to **Lockton,** with its restored 13th century church, and the picturesque hill-top village of **Levisham.** Set round a green, it has at its head a maypole and the Horse-shoe Inn which also serves as the village store and post office. A further 2½ miles take the main road past the **Hole of Horcum,** a vast natural hollow formed by the action of springs wearing away the soft clay below the limestone beds. There is no truth in the legend that it was dug by a giant who used the excavated material to form the curiously isolated mound of Blakey Topping, a half-hour's walk to the east! The Hole of Horcum, which has become a popular hang gliding centre, is best seen from the top of **Saltersgate Bank** where a car park has been provided. From here the view extends northwards over Lockton High Moor, past the Saltersgate Inn with its 'perpetual' peat fire, to the Fylingdales Early Warning Station and its famous 'golf balls'.

Eastwards from Pickering towards Scarborough, the first settlement is

Newton-on-Rawcliffe, a hill-top village north of Pickering. *(J.J. Thomlinson)*

Thornton Dale (often but incorrectly referred to as Thornton-le-Dale). It has been acclaimed the most attractive village in Yorkshire and thus can get very overcrowded at weekends. In the main street many of the houses look as if they have not changed for a hundred years, their low pantiled roofs and small windows radiating an air of Victorian calm and respectability. At the east end of the street a large mansion was once the home of the Hill family, Lords of the Manor, and is now an hotel. At the cross-roads in the village is the market cross and a pair of stocks, whilst Maltongate has a series of bridges spanning Thornton Beck. Upstream on the north side of the main road, a thatched cottage beside the beck must be one of the most photographed buildings in England. The stroll along the path leads to a ford and a bridge over the water near the mill.

The village of Thornton Dale should not be confused with the valley of the same name which contains the picture-postcard hamlet of **Ellerburn.** This is a delightful place with its small group of cottages facing on to a beck and an old Norman church—with a 10th century wheelhead cross and a crucifix cross of the 11th century—nestling in a hollow. The cafe in the hamlet offers an opportunity to eat and drink beside the stream.

Another road heading north out of Thornton Dale climbs on to the moors to link up with the A169 from Pickering to Whitby. Part way along is the turn-off on the right for Low Dalby and the start of the **Forest Drive,** described in the chapter on 'The Forests of the North York Moors'. Three miles along the Drive is the car park for the Bridestones, a series of large weathered rock outcrops which can be reached by a nature walk arranged by the National Trust and the Yorkshire Naturalists' Trust.

The Drive emerges from the trees close to the hamlet of Bickley, from where the road continues through Langdale End and along the valley of the

Derwent to **Hackness,** a beautiful village set alongside Lowdales Beck. Hackness Hall, a Georgian house built by John Carr of York, is the seat of Lord Derwent.

A circular route back to Thornton Dale or Pickering can be completed by a stimulating drive through **Troutsdale,** the road climbing to a height of almost 700 feet near Cockmoor Hall, close to which is a large car park with a splendid view back over the valley. The road then descends to the A170 from Scarborough to Pickering at Snainton. A longer alternative is to continue south-east from Hackness through the richly wooded **Forge Valley,** a place very popular with holidaymakers in Scarborough which lies just three miles to the east. This time the main road is joined at **West Ayton,** with its remains of a castle once owned by the Evers family, and the return westwards is through **Brompton**—where in 1802 William Wordsworth married Mary Hutchinson.

The broad heather-covered expanses of the North York Moors as seen at Old Wife's Neck, Fylingdales. (*Stanhope White*)

The Esk Valley

THE Esk Valley and its numerous tributary dales contain some of the finest scenery in the North York Moors National Park. Motorists should be warned that the area also has some of the steepest hills in Britain, one of the special attractions of Eskdale being that it has no continuous road along the valley floor and one has to keep dodging up and down the slopes to get from village to village. It is in fact best seen from the windows of the diesel trains which link Whitby with Middlesbrough and twist their way through the dale on a most attractive single-line railway. There are stations at Ruswarp, Sleights, Grosmont (change for the North Yorkshire Moors Railway), Egton, Glaisdale, Lealholm, Danby, Castleton Moor, Commondale, and, just beyond the watershed, Kildale and Battersby, the latter being reached in slightly under an hour from Whitby. En route the line crosses the river Esk eighteen times!

Many motorists exploring the Esk Valley start from Whitby and follow the A169 Pickering road across the river to **Sleights,** nestling at the foot of infamous Blue Bank which climbs from just above sea level to almost a thousand feet. It is worth going part way up the bank and turning left to the lovely hamlet of **Littlebeck,** beyond which are the Falling Foss Forest Trail and the May Beck Farm Trail. Best reached from the Ruswarp - Scarborough road, these are more fully described under 'The Forests of the North York Moors'.

A right turn in Sleights leads along Eskdaleside to **Grosmont;** a former centre of iron manufacture, it today attracts many visitors as the northern terminus and motive power headquarters of the North Yorkshire Moors Railway. A 3½ mile Historical Railway Trail, which can be walked one way and covered by train in the other direction, links Grosmont with Goathland.

A typical and most interesting moors village, **Goathland** is reached by leaving the Whitby - Pickering road on the heights of Sleights Moor. It lies in a green depression but the moors are never far away. They spill themselves between the houses as reed-strewn commons which are kept mown by sheep. Goathland is an old village; it had a church in 1100 and the King's bailiff built a mill in 1210. The surroundings are exceptional and include a number of waterfalls in most attractive settings. A footpath leads down to the 45ft high Mallyan Spout, while to the west is Nelly Ayre Foss and to the north on Eller Beck the falls of Ark Force and Thomason Foss. The latter two are most easily reached from **Darnholm,** a picturesque

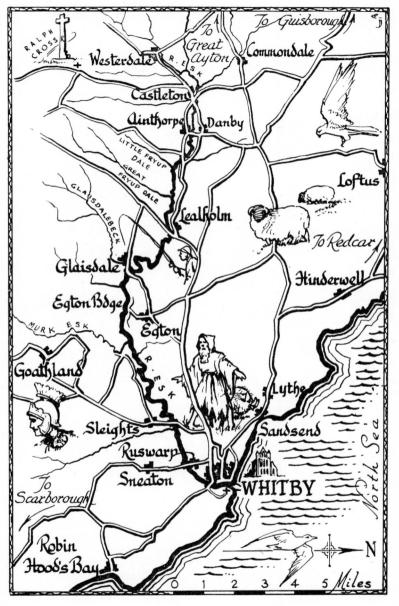

Map by E. Jeffrey.

Above: The rolling expanse of Little Fryupdale, with the Esk Valley in the distance.

Right: Danby High Moor, with the open road slicing through acre upon acre of heather. (both *North York Moors National Park*)

place with a ford and stepping stones. Even more attractive is **Beck Hole**, a mile to the north-west and reached down a 1 in 3 hill, which has its houses clustering round the village green and an inn with a sign painted by Algernon Newton. It lies at the foot of the former rope-worked incline on the original course of the Whitby & Pickering Railway.

Beyond Grosmont the road crosses the Esk at its confluence with the Murk Esk and climbs to **Egton**, a hill top village noted for its annual Gooseberry Show in August. A left-turn descends steeply to **Egton Bridge** and its well-wooded surroundings; at the side of the Horseshoe Hotel stepping stones cross the river via an island in the middle. The Stape road, climbing high on to the moors before descending to a pretty picnic site at Wheeldale Gill, provides the easiest means of reaching the well-preserved section of **Roman road** on Wheeldale Moor. It ran from the Roman fortress at Malton via Cawthorne Camp to Lease Rigg near Grosmont and probably continued to the coast.

Glaisdale, the next village up-river, is noted for its exquisite pack-horse bridge bearing the initials T.F. and the date 1619. The initials are said to belong to Thomas Ferris who reputedly built the bridge after being separated from his sweetheart by the swollen waters of the Esk. It is situated near the railway station. On the north-west side of Glaisdale (the valley as opposed to the village) the flagged causeway once used by pannier ponies heading over the moors to Rosedale can clearly be seen.

Minor roads run along the south side of Eskdale before crossing the river to **Lealholm,** a scattered village with a quoits pitch on the green. Opposite are the twin valleys of **Great and Little Fryup Dale,** split by the curiously named Fairy Cross Plain. At the foot of the smaller dale is **Danby Castle,** erected by the de Latimer family in the 14th century. Now partly ruined and partly converted into a farmhouse, it nevertheless still retains two massive towers, a vaulted dungeon, high walls with fireplaces and window openings, a spiral staircase and many other medieval features. Katherine Parr, one of Henry VIII's wives who kept her head, once lived in the castle. It was originally approached by Duck Bridge, a delightful pack-horse structure in a sylvan setting.

Almost directly opposite the castle on the north side of the river (alongside the road from Lealholm to Danby via Houlsyke) is **Danby Lodge,** a former shooting lodge which has now been converted into the National Park Centre. Inside is a series of static displays on life on the moorlands, geology, natural history and other subjects connected with the

area. Film shows and talks are given, and there is a Tourist Information Centre and cafe. Nature trails are laid out in the extensive grounds which stretch down towards the Esk. Immediately east of the Centre a side road climbs to **Danby Beacon**, 981 feet above sea level and one of the best viewpoints on the North York Moors. The panorama covers the Esk Valley, the northern dales and moors and out to the North Sea.

Danby is much visited for its church which stands remotely at the entrance to beautiful **Danby Dale** and still retains its 15th century tower. In the churchyard is an ancient cross of traditional wheelhead design as well as many interesting gravestones, including that of Canon J. C. Atkinson, Vicar of Danby for 53 years from 1847 to 1900, who wrote the classic book 'Forty Years in a Moorland Parish'. At the head of the dale is **Botton Village**, a community of handicapped people and helpers. Run by the Camphill Village Trust, the centre includes four farms and a number of workshops for crafts such as enamelling, glass engraving, metalwork, woodwork and printing. Visitors are welcome, a coffee bar and gift shop being open daily.

The centre of the upper reaches of the Esk Valley is **Castleton**, a large village little more than a mile west of Danby. It is the starting point for perhaps the most splendid road on the North York Moors which immediately climbs up the hog-backed hill of Castleton Rigg, giving from the almost knife-edged ridge some plunging views into both Danby Dale and Westerdale. It continues to climb to a summit of just under 1,400 feet at Rosedale Head, near which are the two Ralph's Crosses, before gradually descending along Blakey Ridge to Hutton-le-Hole.

The river Esk rises at Esklets at the very head of **Westerdale** and somewhat surprisingly little more than a mile from the top part of Farndale. Near Westerdale village is a paved causeway crossing an ancient ribbed pack-horse bridge, over restored in 1874. The last house in the settlement going south has a quaint monument in its private garden to a mariner who 'wrecked at lenth' retired here in 1727 and raised the structure in thanks for his survival. The road over to Kildale descends to Baysdale Beck where there is a good picnic site beside the stream.

Danby Castle, the ruined stronghold on the south side of the Esk Valley.
(Elizabeth Gray)

Cleveland Hills
and Plain

THE North York Moors in many ways look more dramatic from a distance than at close quarters. This is certainly the case when travelling over the Cleveland Plain from Thirsk to Guisborough via Stokesley and Great Ayton, the dramatic western and later northern edge of the Moors dominating the skyline for mile after mile.

The Guisborough road parts company with the A19 from York to Teesside at the **Cleveland Tontine,** an hotel built in 1804 by a shareholding lottery company of local investors, the ultimate survivor to be the winner of the property! It was a famous stopping point in coaching days. Immediately to the south-east at the end of a track off the A19 is **Mount Grace Priory,** founded in 1398 and today the best preserved Carthusian monastery in Britain. The monks lived in virtual isolation in individual cells, one of which has been restored to its former condition.

Osmotherley, also reached off the A19, is attractively set on the hillside facing south and has in its centre a market cross and stone market hall. It has a church with a 15th century tower and fragments of Saxon crosses in the porch. Historically more significant is one of the earliest Methodist chapels in England; reached down a narrow passage opposite the market cross, it is inscribed with the date 1754 over the doorway and was probably built shortly after John Wesley preached in the village. Completing the ecclesiastical connections is Lady Chapel, built in the early 16th century but with many later additions. A half hour's walk away, it is open all the year and offers marvellous views over the Vale of York.

Minor roads tempt the inquisitive motorist out of Osmotherley either to Hawnby (see 'Helmsley and the Hambletons') or to Swainby via **Scarth Nick.** This narrow pass between the hills—a dramatic example of an Ice Age overflow channel—was traversed by the **Hambleton Drove Road,** an ancient highway along which Scottish drovers brought their cattle south to the markets and fairs for sale. After crossing the river Tees at Yarm and climbing on to the moors via Scarth Nick, it ran roughly south for 15 miles along the western escarpment of the hills to Sutton Bank where it forked, one way continuing via Coxwold to York and the other along Ampleforth High Street to Malton. A booklet on the road is published by the North York Moors National Park. **Sheepwash,** on the south side of the Nick, has several parking places and is an attractive and popular picnic spot; it is overlooked by Scarth Wood Moor, the starting point of the Lyke Wake Walk.

The main street of Osmotherley, a village on the north-western edge of the Moors which forms the starting point of the Lyke Wake Walk.
(*Clifford Robinson*)

Swainby is a relatively modern village which grew in the ironstone mining period of Victorian times, overtaking the earlier settlement of **Whorlton** immediately to the east. Here the ruined church of Holy Cross dates from the 12th century and is of considerable interest, the remains including a plain barrel font of Norman design. Whorlton Castle, originally a wooden keep, was replaced in the 14th century by the Meynell family. The outstanding feature is the gate house which displays the family crests.

Carlton-in-Cleveland, like Swainby just off the main road from Cleveland and Tontine to Stokesley, lies alongside Alum Beck—the name a reminder of former quarrying activities. The road through the village continues to Chop Gate at the head of Bilsdale, climbing to almost the 1,000 ft contour during the ascent of **Carlton Bank.** This is perhaps the finest of the readily accessible viewpoints on the northern edge of the Cleveland Hills. It takes in the Teesside conurbation as well as offering a panorama ranging north-westwards towards the Pennines.

Spacious and dignified **Stokesley**, a typical North Yorkshire market town with a predominantly 18th century appearance, is now by-passed. The broad High Street has a green as its west end, whilst other features of interest include the Town Hall, the Shambles and the Butter Market. The parish church of St Peter has a 15th century tower and chancel with a capacious nave of 1771. A pleasant backwater is formed by the infant river Leven which meanders under a stone pack-horse bridge, repaired in 1632 in order to enable the parson to cross into the town and visit the sick!

The road south from Stokesley to Helmsley surmounts the edge of the hills at **Clay Bank**, 842 ft, where there is a Forestry Commission car park and a snack bar. The view extends over the plain to Roseberry Topping. A gateway on the east side of the pass marks the starting point of a bridle-way leading to **Botton Head**, two miles away, the highest point on the North York Moors. On the opposite side of the road steps and a stile take the walker to the 1,304ft top of **Hasty Bank** and on to the Wainstones, a group of eroded sandstone rocks popular with climbers.

From Clay Bank the circumnavigation of the Cleveland escarpment can be continued by returning to the Stokesley bypass or by taking the minor road through **Ingleby Greenhow**, a picturesque village with a long history. The church is of Norman origin with a tower reminiscent of Saxon work; the north arcade piers have some crude animal carvings. Prominent to the south-east of the settlement, on Ingleby Moor, is the course of the incline which was used to lower ironstone wagons from Rosedale down a precipitous descent of almost a thousand feet (see 'Kirkbymoorside and the Southern Dales').

Great Ayton, astride the Stokesley - Guisborough road, retains the atmosphere of a rural settlement despite much modern development. It was here that James Cook, born at Marton-in-Cleveland in 1728, spent his schooldays before trekking east to Staithes to begin a sea-going career that was to end in fame and fortune. The school, rebuilt in 1785, is now a Captain Cook Museum, two rooms devoted to his exploits being reached up an external staircase. Cook's father built a cottage in the village which was removed to Fitzroy Gardens, Melbourne, Australia, where it too is now a Cook museum. In its place stands an obelisk of stones from Point Hicks the first part of Australia to be sighted by Captain Cook on April 20th 1770. On top of the 1,064ft Easby Moor is the **Captain Cook Monument** erected in 1827 and reached by taking the road through Little Ayton and driving up to Gribdale Gate. The path from this point runs alongside forestry plantations.

It is less than two miles as the crow flies from Easby Moor to **Roseberry Topping,** thirteen feet lower but infinitely more impressive as it is isolated from the surrounding moorlands. It was in fact once the higher of the two peaks but subsidence resulting from medieval iron workings caused this distinction to be lost. The almost volcanic shape is due to erosion of the surrounding land, the hill bearing an Oolitic cap which protects the underlying Lias. Most easily climbed from Newton-under-Roseberry, the peak has long been popular with countrygoers and is today the starting point of the White Rose Walk.

Guisborough, now a dormitory for Teesside, makes a good base to explore the northern fringe of the North York Moors. Its greatest glory is the solitary but majestic east end of the Augustinian priory of St Mary, founded in 1119 by Robert de Brus and once one of the wealthiest monasteries in the north. Standing almost 100 ft high, the remains have a central window with a carved surround of elaborate foliage displaying the shields of the founders. The town has a broad, cobble-fringed main street with some attractive buildings above the modern shop facades—a market is held on Thursdays and Saturdays. It is worth visiting the Chapel Beck Gallery which combines an art gallery, museum and interpretive centre; there are changing displays of artistic and historic interest.

The Wainstones, a group of eroded rocks at the western end of Hasty Bank, easily reached from Clay Bank on the Stokesley to Helmsley road.
(Alec Wright)

Carlton Bank, one of the best viewpoints on the North York Moors.
(*Alec Wright*)

Scarth Wood Moor, overlooking the Cleveland plain north of Osmotherley, is traversed by both the Cleveland Way and the Lyke Wake Walk.
(*Bill Cowley*)

Whitby and
the Coast

THE North York Moors end abruptly and dramatically in the east with one of the finest stretches of 'heritage' coastline in the country. The coast is described only briefly in this guide as it is fully covered in other Dalesman publications, notably the 'White Rose' guide **Yorkshire Coast,** as well as **Exploring the Yorkshire Coast** and individual guides on **Whitby, Robin Hood's Bay** and **Scarborough.**

*   *   *

Whitby is undoubtedly one of the most popular holiday resorts in northern England. With its natural charms, the neighbouring hills and moorland and the river Esk which winds its way peacefully to the coast, the town is ideally located. The Esk divides Whitby into two parts with the old town, a picturesque arrangement of rooftops and ginnels, resting on the east side of the river. It is here that the well-known 199 steps may be found. Locally referred to as the Church Stairs, they lead to the ancient parish church of St Mary which dates from 1110. The building alone speaks much of its history as numerous alterations result in a unique combination of architectural styles. Close to the church, and equally exposed on top of the 200ft cliff, stand the ruins of Whitby Abbey. Founded in 657 by Hilda, the daughter of the king of Northumbria, the abbey flourished until the dissolution of the monasteries by Henry VIII. The remains are chiefly from the 13th and 14th centuries.

The modern part of Whitby—the new town—is situated on the West Cliff with all the amenities required to make up an active resort. Aside a variety of entertainments and shops lies Whitby's two-mile stretch of sands. Here, sport may be enjoyed alongside boating, fishing and bathing. As a fishing town, Whitby remains dominated by its well-known harbour, where visitors gather to watch the locals at their work. A swing bridge links the two halves of the town so that the 'atmospheric' past is kept distinct from the present. In the spa grounds overlooking the two stone piers stands a statue erected in memory of Captain Cook, who sailed from Whitby in the locally-built 'Resolution'.

Sandsend, appropriately named for it is the point where Whitby sands end, is best described as a seaside village. This attractive settlement enjoys coastal scenery among a wealth of greenery. Wooded glens and twisting paths surround the houses which stand protected from the sea by a sea wall. Close to Sandsend is Mulgrave Castle—a notable monument

41

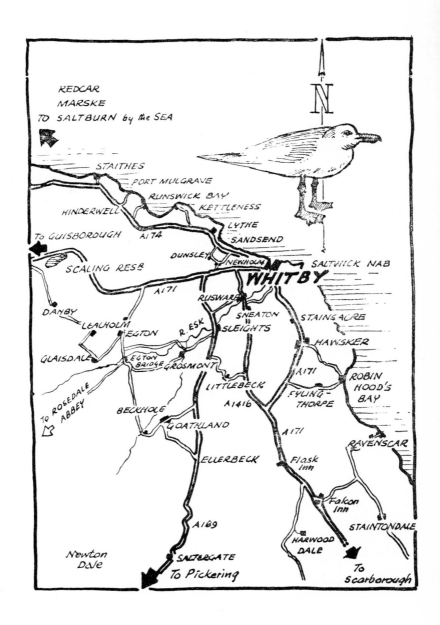

Staithes, clustering at the foot of the cliffs, epitomises the old fishing villages of the Yorkshire coast (*Alec Wright*)

surrounded by trees, lying only a short distance inland. The castle should be approached by East Row Drive where there is a car park.

Although once a fishing community, **Runswick Bay** is now essentially a holiday centre. Lying in a remote corner of the coastline and hidden from the tops by the rugged cliffs, the bay remains mysterious and secluded. Cottages at Runswick stand huddled side by side, balancing quite precariously on the sides of the cliffs! A sea wall has recently been erected as over the years many houses have been washed away by the tide. Of particular interest is the obvious lack of roads. Cottages are linked by narrow passageways and paths which ensures that an intimate community is maintained. The Bay proves tempting for a variety of artists, understandably intrigued by Runswick's aesthetic appeal. Though uncommercialised, the settlement caters well for visitors with a small collection of shops, hotels and car parks in both the upper and lower parts of the village.

The somewhat plain approach to **Staithes** gives little indication that a quaint old fishing community lies beyond. The cottages are set either side of a deep valley where Roxby Beck runs into the sea. Once a fishing port of much importance, the village has a history closely associated with its ancient harbour and the days of smuggling. It was here that Captain Cook served his apprenticeship as a draper before leaving for Whitby and a life on the seas. Sadly, all that remain to remind the visitor of busier days are a few small boats and the tales of retired fisherfolk. At Staithes, a car park is provided near the Captain Cook Inn. It is recommended that visitors use this, as parking space in the village is very limited.

Robin Hood's Bay, or Baytown as it is known by locals, is characterised by its picturesque assortment of red pantile roofs and quietly smoking chimney pots. Not unlike Runswick, cottages are built almost vertically against the steep and lofty cliffside. As with many of these coastal settlements, Baytown developed initially as a well-populated fishing town and more particularly played a significant part in the smuggling activities of the 17th and 18th centuries. It is said that many of the cottages are connected by secret passageways where fisherfolk once stored a variety of forbidden goods. Steeped in the secrecy and wonder of local folk lore, Baytown has become a legend in itself, attracting artists and visitors eager to explore hidden ginnels and rediscover something of the village's adventurous past. Often compared with Clovelly in the West Country, it is believed that Baytown was used by Robin Hood and his men as a retreat during difficult times. Visitors will find a car park in the upper, more modern part of the village. Access beyond this point is possible only on foot.

Dominated by the well-known Raven Hall Hotel, **Ravenscar** lies on top of a 600ft headland and commands extensive views of the area's coastal scenery as well as across the North Sea. A pathway leads down to the shore from this point, providing opportunity to study the geology and wildlife along this section of coastline. The hotel grounds are open to non-residents at a small charge. Here one may walk along terraces overlooking the sea or take advantage of the open-air swimming pool. Ravenscar is the finishing point of the popular Lyke Wake Walk, which starts at Osmotherley and covers 40 miles over the North York Moors.

Opposite: Hesketh as viewed from Boltby Scar, just south of the road down Sneck Yate Bank. (*Bill Cowley*)

Discovering the Moors
by Car

Three recommended drives

1. Daffodils and Conifers: Eskdale - Rosedale - Farndale - Thornton-le-dale - Forest Drive.

Based on Scarborough, 79 miles.

THIS tour takes the Scarborough holidaymaker into the heart of the North York Moors National Park. On its concluding stages the motorist can drive for some ten miles through tall pines on the increasingly popular Forest Drive.

Leave Scarborough by A171 and pass through Scalby with its attractive gardens to Burniston and Cloughton, which has many old stone houses. Continue along A171 for some nine miles past Harwood Dale Forest and over the eastern fringe of Fylingdales Moor. A worthwhile detour is to

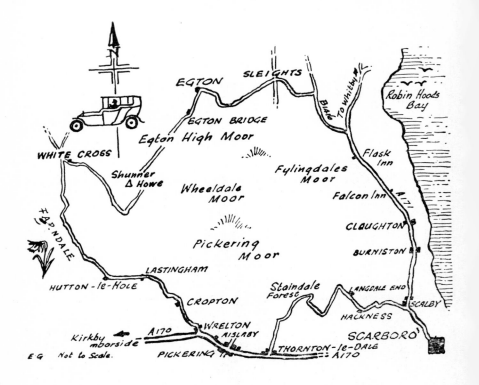

Robin Hood's Bay, the beautiful little fishing village perched on the edge of the North Sea cliffs. The red-roofed cottages, the cobbles and the lobster pots of the Bay have been vividly portrayed in **Three Fevers** and **Phantom Lobster,** classic writings by the late Leo Walmsley.

Return along A171 for a short distance, and then turn right onto B1416. Then take the second turning left, a sharp one, and then first right. After a mile Ugglebarnby with its interesting church is reached. A steep descent leads to Sleights and Eskdale. Turn left onto A169 and almost immediately right, the turning being signposted Grosmont. From Sleights a detour could be made into Whitby, or indeed the tour could be started from there.

Grosmont was formerly noted for its ironstone workings, which were of some considerable extent. Continue straight through the village, across the River Esk and up a very steep hill to Egton. The village and its surrounding district is of great interest to antiquarians by reason of its ancient graves, and the many bronze and jet ornaments which have been discovered. In the church the almsbox is made from timber which came from Nelson's flagship, the **Victory**.

Turn left in the village and a long descent leads to Egton Bridge where the River Esk is crossed again. Follow the Rosedale signposts. After passing through some very beautiful woods, the road leaves the Esk valley and gradually climbs onto the moors, reaching a height of nearly 1,100 feet. For six miles the road is unfenced and there are some magnificent views down into Glaisdale and over miles of heather-covered moor. There are some interesting tumuli two miles from Egton Bridge and near the summit are a large number of old coal pits. Not far away to the east is a chalybeate spring.

The road suddenly drops into Rosedale Abbey. The second half of the village's name is a reminder that a nunnery was founded here in the 12th century by Robert de Stuteville. Very few traces of it now remain. Do not take the Spaunton Moor road as it includes an almost impossibly steep climb of 1 in 3, but turn right in the village, and after a mile right again. It is a very long climb out of Rosedale but eventually open moor is again reached. At a junction almost 1,400 feet above sea level at Rosedale Head turn left. There are many interesting antiquities nearby. The road continues to cross open moor, passing Blakey House, one of England's highest inns. After two miles turn right and descend very steeply into Farndale, nationally famous for its daffodils.

Turn left in Church Houses, the first hamlet reached, and after some three miles the road climbs out of the dale and then drops into Hutton-le-Hole, one of the prettiest villages in the National Park, with its haphazardly scattered houses. Sheep can often be seen grazing among the buildings. Take the left fork on entering the village and after a few yards turn left again. It is a short journey across a bracken covered common and through woodland to Lastingham, a village with a long history. Its church is one of the most interesting in Yorkshire.

Turn left and following the Pickering signposts cross the River Seven and climb into Cropton. It is only a short detour to the famous Cawthorn Camps. Continue to follow the Pickering signposts, and shortly after leaving the village a magnificent view opens up over the Vale of Pickering to the Howardian Hills and the Wolds. At Wrelton turn left onto A170 and pass through Aislaby with its many old cottages and Middleton with its Saxon church to Pickering. This is an old town worth more than a passing glance. The church, famous for its wall paintings, and the castle should both be examined.

Pickering is close to Flamingo Park Zoo at Kirkby Misperton, which is reached by taking the A169 Malton road and turning first right. The zoo is a must for all children. The speciality is sea mammals—these include whales, dolphins and elephant seals, and there is a very large collection of waterfowl.

Return to Pickering and follow A170 to Thornton-le-Dale, another very beautiful village. Turn left at the cross roads towards Whitby and after little more than a mile look out for a turning right signposted "Low Dalby only." This leads to the Forest Drive, on which, through the kindness of

The showrooms of Robert Thompsons', the woodcarvers of Kilburn. Note in the foreground the stacks of oak seasoning and in the background the White Horse. (*Clifford Robinson*)

the Forestry Commission, the visitor can enjoy Canadian surroundings and see almost every kind of conifer at close quarters. The Drive ends at Bickley, and after passing through the hamlet of Darncombe the finely sited village of Hackness is reached. The road runs through Hackness Hall park, with its lake, to Scalby and back into Scarborough. An alternative route is through the Forge Valley via East Ayton.

2. West from Whitby: Fryup Dale - Westerdale - Bransdale -Riccall Dale - Kirkdale - Goathland.

Based on Whitby, 80 miles.

LITTLE dales and steep climbs are the essence of a run which includes such diverse features as a seaside village, a ridge road, a Saxon church and the extraordinary Hole of Horcum. Leave the most interesting of Yorkshire's coastal towns by A174 for Sandsend, a mini-resort which is well-named for here the Whitby sands end and towering cliffs stretching as far as Saltburn begin. Lythe Bank, climbing from sea level to 450-ft., has a more notorious reputation than it deserves, but nevertheless care is needed. The church at Lythe, isolated from the village and having massive buttresses and some beautiful woodwork, is well worth a visit. Turn left in the village for Ugthorpe.

Turn left at the junction with A171 and first right to follow a narrow road which drops down to Lealholm in Eskdale. This was an ancient track from Pickering to Whitby and alongside it runs a paved pannier way. It was here that the Rev. J. C. Atkinson, famous for his book **Forty Years in a Moorland Parish**, watched wagons laden with freestone blocks waiting in turn for haulage up the hill by teams consisting of ten oxen and ten draught horses. At Lealholm, a jumble of red-roofed houses, cross the narrow gorge of the Esk by a one-arched bridge and follow the signposts to enter Great Fryup Dale, now becoming noted for its field studies centre. The delightfully named Fairy Cross Plain provides a link with Little Fryup Dale, only 1½ miles long and surely one of the shortest dales in Yorkshire. At its foot is Danby Castle, which is part ruin and part farmhouse and retains little of its ancient splendour.

Continue to Castleton, where the church has the carvings of the Mouse Man on its sturdy benches and organ screen. For such a rural area the road junctions at the west end of the village are of bewildering complexity and careful map or signpost reading is required to enter Westerdale. The village of the same name is notable for the Ancient Mariner's Memorial to Thomas Bulmer and the architecturally incongruous youth hostel—a combination of a Bavarian castle, an Elizabethan manor house, an octagon and a chapel. One mile north of the village is Hob Hole, a perfect picnic spot.

The route climbs steeply out of the valley to join the well-used and important ridge road from Castleton to Hutton-le-Hole; there are wonderful views of heather moors and the upper reaches of Rosedale. Turn right at Little Blakey to drop steeply down to Farndale. Follow the road down the west side of the valley and pass through Low Mill to reach Gillamoor. Go to the east end of the churchyard for one of Yorkshire's most impressive views—the river Dove winding through the green valley to a background of heathery moors made mosaic-like by a network of tracks and tarmac roads. Turn right and pass over great expanses of open moor before arriving at lonely Cockayne Church in little-visited Bransdale.

Bear right as the road swings southwards. More open heath follows before the route drops gently into Riccal Dale and almost immediately climbs steeply out of this virtually deserted valley. Civilisation is regained at Helmsley, where the castle, the church and Duncombe Park are all worthy of examination. Rievaulx Abbey lies 2½ miles away to the northwest.

Go east from Helmsley on A170 to Beadlam, pronounced "beedlam," and Nawton. Where the main road abruptly swings right keep straight on for Kirkdale Minster, an architectural jewel in a secluded valley. Inside the porch is the unique sundial with its Saxon inscription. There is a legend that the church was intended to be built at Stone Cross but the masonry was moved by fairies.

Cross a picturesque watersplash to reach Kirkbymoorside, a busy market

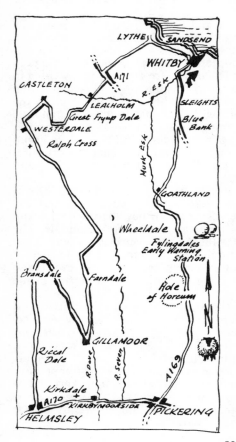

Further motor runs are described in **Explore Yorkshire by Car— The North York Moors,** *a Dalesman paperback.*

town where the Slingsby Hunt have their kennels. The town's most famous inhabitant was George Villiers, 2nd Duke of Buckingham and one of the most dazzling courtiers of all time. He died in poverty in a house overlooking the Toll Booth, the last words he wrote being: "The world and I shake hands, for I dare affirm we are heartily weary of each other."

A170 leads to Pickering, a town noted for its stately castle and the magnificent 15th century wall paintings in the church. The route north from Pickering is on one of the most exhilarating class "A" roads in Britain with its gentle curves, generally easy gradients and sweeping views across vast expanses of moorland. One of the astonishing sights is the Hole of Horcum, a stupendous green bowl in the hills and traditionally said to have been dug by a giant. Nearby is Saltergate and the **Wagon and Horses Inn** with its peat fire which has never been allowed to go out.

Pass close to Fylingdales Early Warning Station and its three white globes which can be regarded either as eyesores or modern architecture at its best. Turn left for a look at Goathland, a village which spreads itself over a plateau and has long been popular for country holidays. Its river is the Murk Esk, the name probably being derived from the old Norse word, "Myrkur," meaning dark or mysterious. On the tributary of West Beck is the 70 ft. high waterfall of Mallyan Spout, and nearby Wheeldale Moor has an excavated portion of Roman road over a mile long. Return to A169 for Sleights and Whitby.

3. Escape from Teesside: Bilsdale - Commondale - Eskdale -Runswick Bay - Staithes.

Based on Stokesley, 57 miles.

STOKESLEY has always dominated the Cleveland area and it is to this spacious and tidy town that the tourists and day visitors set their sights from wide areas of North Yorkshire and Durham. While the town itself has many attractions it is to the countryside and coast beyond that the cars are bound.

Leave Stokesley on the A172 Thirsk road and pass through Carlton, a wooded village set in the shadow of the Cleveland Hills. Turn left after three miles and climb steeply up Carlton Banks on a well surfaced but narrow and twisting road which reaches a height of almost 1,000 ft. On a clear day the view from this point must be one of the finest in Yorkshire. Spread below is the rich plain extending to the urban sprawl of Teesside. The hills of Durham rise beyond. Roseberry Topping and Easby Moor with the monument to Captain Cook on the summit are to the right, with the outline of the Pennines far to the left.

Continue over Cringle Moor to join the B1257 Helmsley-Stokesley road at Chop Gate—the red pantiled village better known as "Chop Yat." Turn left, ascending to the brow of Hasty Bank, where a narrow road branches right to Ingleby Greenhow. The small Norman church partly rebuilt

51

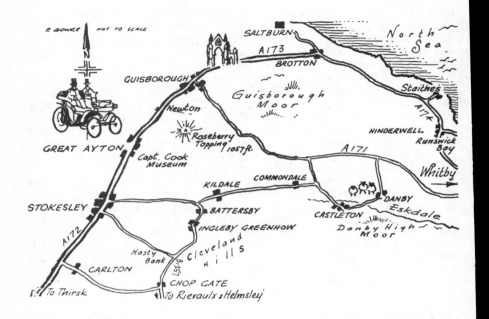

200 years ago is the feature of another village which nestles at the foot of the steep bare slopes of the Clevelands.

Pass through Battersby, a village notable only for its past importance as a railway junction, and continue on to Kildale, a former Viking settlement situated in the valley of the River Leven. Arable land around the villages soon gives way to moorland, and sheep become the dominant feature of a now rugged landscape. Commondale, in its hollow amid the hills, is now little more than a hamlet, all evidence of its once thriving brick and pipe works having gone.

Climbing steeply away from Commondale take the first turn to the right, for Castleton. This straggling village has open moorland at its western extremity, gradually giving way to arable pastures and the River Esk, here not many miles from its source. A left turn in Castleton and two miles away is Denby. This is a pleasant open village where sheep wander amid the houses, keeping the broad green verges trim and neatly cropped. Danby Church is famous for the 53 years' service given to it by Canon J. C. Atkinson. A scholarly man, he spent much of his time studying the history and folk-lore of the area.

Leaving Danby, drive three miles over Danby Low Moor to join the A171 Guisborough-Whitby road. Turn right on to this "highway to the coast," but for little more than 5 miles. A signpost denotes a left fork to Hinderwell and Runswick Bay, and within a few minutes there is the first sight

52

of the sea. Runswick Bay is one of the delights of the Yorkshire coast, a unique fishing village clinging to what appears to be a sheer cliff face. The motorist must explore the village on foot, for despite an excellent road to the beach below, this is very clearly marked "For local traffic only." The visitor must leave his car at the cliff top.

Return to Hinderwell and, after two miles on A174, Staithes is reached. Although cars can be taken down to the harbour, this is not advisable. The narrow streets are also steep, and parking is very limited. Staithes is one of the few genuine fishing villages still to be found on the Yorkshire coast with a character all its own. Inns abound near the quayside, including the aptly named **Cod and Lobster**.

Rejoining A174, make for Brotton, a village only three miles from Saltburn. Turn left on to A173 and drive through undulating country to Guisborough, a splendid market town dominated by its ruined Priory. Between Guisborough and Great Ayton the road, at Newton, comes almost to the foot of Roseberry Topping (1,057 ft.). This is a fine opportunity for the energetic to climb this unique mountain which stands alone and isolated from the main Cleveland heights.

Great Ayton is another village with direct connections with Captain Cook. It was here that he spent his boyhood. The explorer's former school-room has been converted into a small museum. The village, with its attractive greens and the River Leven flowing for a mile through its length, makes a pleasant halt. From here it is but a short drive back to Stokesley.

Walks on the
North York Moors

White Horse of Kilburn

Starting Point: Car park at the summit of Sutton Bank on the Thirsk-Helmsley road (A170), 4 miles from Thirsk, G.R. 514830.

Distance: 6½ miles.

FINE views westwards across the Vale of York to the Yorkshire Dales and the Pennines are obtained during this walk, which is one of the most varied in the National Park.

From the car park, cross over the main road and follow the footpath which begins almost opposite the junction with the by-road to Cold Kirby and Old Byland. The path leads to a viewpoint indicator and then continues along the edge of the steep escarpment for 1¼ miles. At the end of the path you will reach the White Horse of Kilburn, identifiable at this stage only as a large white area immediately below on the right, from which both turf and vegetation have been cleared. Directly beyond this, descend the hillside by a series of steps to a car park clearly visible below on the right.

Continue descending the hillside, either by a series of hairpin bends in the minor road, or by a path which follows the left-hand side of the road, until you reach a steep hill sign. Immediately beyond this, follow the farm road branching off to the right and, where it turns left to Acre House Farm, keep straight on along a grassy track between hedges, ultimately passing through a gate into a forestry plantation. Follow the track into the Forestry Commission land, avoiding a grass track forking off to the left, until the main access track comes in from the left.

Keep straight on along this track to take the left fork at the bottom of the hill. Your way winds round the side of Hood Hill and, as the path bears left, a field and boundary fence are immediately on your right. As soon as the boundary fence moves away from the track, follow the fence down-hill to pass through a wicket gate into a field. Walk down the field towards Hood Grange (the ancient stone farmhouse, a quarter of a mile away in the valley bottom). Just before you reach the farm, turn left along the side of the beck for a short distance and then turn right to reach the farm access road by the farm gate. Turn left along the road, and follow it round a right and left-hand bend until the main Thirsk-Helmsley road is reached.

Turn sharp right along the main road, and at the top of a short incline after about 100 yards, turn left to follow the access road to Cleaves Farm. On reaching the farm buildings, pass through the gate in front of you at the far end, and follow the rough track across the field and then go through another gate. In front you will see a third gate. Do not go through this, but bear slightly to the left, and follow the hedge towards a fourth gate between some trees. The way is now clear to Cleaves House in

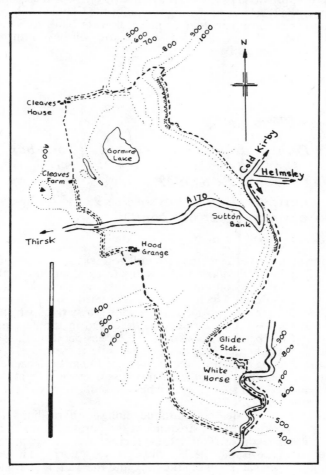

front of you. On reaching the boundary of the property, turn right over a stile by a gate and then immediately left. Continue along the edge of the grounds to reach a minor road at the side of a barn.

Turn right along the road, and after a quarter mile a cottage with an elegantly cut hawthorn tree is reached on the left, and notices state that you have reached the end of vehicular access. Immediately after passing the cottage, bear slightly right along the 'Bridlepath to Gormire'. After about 100 yards from the cottage, a narrower path will be seen bearing left as the main path bears right. It is signposted 'Thirlby Bank Bridleway' on a small ground-level sign. Follow it gradually uphill; there are a number of deviations but, provided that you always choose one which ascends, the top will obviously be reached. At the highest point the Cleveland Way is joined as it follows the escarpment edge from Sneck Yate Bank to Sutton Bank. Turn right, and in three-quarters of a mile you will have returned to the car park from which you started.

The Hole of Horcum

Starting Point: Car park near the A.A. 'phone box, ½ mile south of the Saltersgate Inn on the A169 Whitby to Pickering road, G.R. 853937.

Public Transport: United bus service 92, Whitby-Pickering -Malton passes the starting point.

Distance: 5½ or 7 miles.

WALK downhill along the main road until you reach the angle of the hairpin bend. Turn left and follow a wide stony track along the northern edge of the Hole of Horcum, continuing over heather moorland past Seavy Pond to reach Dundale Pond, which is two miles from the road. If you wish to shorten the walk, turn sharply left on to a wide grassy track which descends into a shallow valley, then continue as described in the next paragraph. Otherwise use the path signposted 'R.A. Extension Route', which goes diagonally to the right and leads to a gate and stile at the end of 1 enclosed lane. Continue along the lane to the Horse Shoe Inn at Levisham and return by the lane on the other side of the inn. Cross over the stile at the far end of the lane and proceed along a path which goes diagonally to the right and joins the path from Dundale Pond.

The path from Dundale Pond continues alongside a tree-lined ravine and, if you keep to the right of the streamlet at the bottom, you will come to a wooden footpath signpost. Turn left here, cross over the streamlet and the footbridge over Levisham Beck, which is very narrow at this point. Continue along the path between the beck and the wall, then walk over the

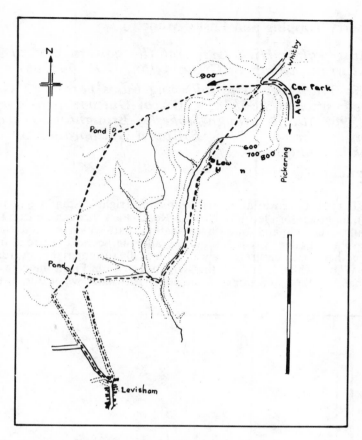

fields to Low Horcum Farm, keeping halfway between the beck and the
wood on your right. Pass immediately to the left of the farm and follow a
wide grassy track to a stile and gate. The track then continues straight ahead
and climbs up the hillside to join the main road at the hairpin bend. Turn
right to reach the car park.

Roseberry Topping and Easby Moor

Starting Point: High Green at the eastern end of High Street in the village of Great Ayton, G.R. 563106.

Public Transport: The following buses pass High Green: United services 280/281, Redcar-Guisborough-Stokesley and 290, Middlesbrough-Stokesley-Broughton; Cleveland Transit service 71, Saltburn-Guisborough-Stokesley (weekdays only).

Distance: 6½ miles.

LEAVE High Green in an easterly direction (right if standing facing the shops), and then turn left into Newton Road. Pass through an iron gate in the wall on the right and follow a well-defined path which passes to the right of Cleveland Lodge. Cross the railway and the access road to a lineside cottage, then continue straight ahead, eventually turning right towards Cliff Ridge Wood, which is entered through an iron gate. From the gate, climb diagonally to the right along an indistinct path and, when this turns left

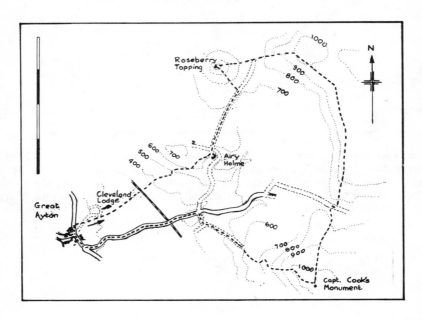

along a fence at the top, climb over the stile and walk across the field, passing to the left of Airy Holme Farm. Turn right over a cattle grid, then turn left and follow a cart track to a gate at the base of Roseberry Topping, beyond which you turn left and climb to the summit.

From the summit, walk eastwards along the ridge to near the end, where you bear left and descend by an obvious path which soon follows the left-hand side of a wall. At the bottom, keep straight on uphill and, after passing through a wicket gate in a wall, continue along the wall on your right. About a mile later, cross over the minor road at Gribdale Gate and ascend by a wide forest track to Captain Cook's Monument on the summit of Easby Moor.

If you stand with your back to the inscription on the base of the monument, you will see a path going diagonally to the right. Continue along this path; after a short distance it follows a wall and, when the wall makes a right-angled bend, go diagonally to the left and enter a forest. Follow the path downhill through the forest and go through a wicket gate at the bottom. Now walk beside the wall on the right, then turn right along a track which soon goes through a gate and becomes an enclosed green lane. Eventually you come to a crossroads, where you turn left and follow the road to a 'T' junction on the outskirts of Great Ayton. To reach High Green, turn right, and then left about 300 yards later.

(*The above walks are from "Walking on the North Moors", a Dalesman book compiled by the Ramblers' Association which describes 25 circular routes in the area*).

Two Long-Distance Walks

The Lyke Wake Walk

THE Lyke Wake Walk probably needs little introduction. As the country's first open challenge walk it has undoubtedly contributed to the fine tradition of long distance walking which now surrounds the North York Moors area. Since Bill Cowley first threw down the gauntlet in **The Dalesman** of August 1955 some 100,000 crossings have been made. The popularity of the walk should not disguise its difficulties and thorough planning and preparation are the hallmarks of success. For those who have not been initiated the walk is a 40 mile traverse of the North York Moors from the most westerly point, near Osmotherley, to the most easterly point at Ravenscar. Those who complete the route within 24 hours qualify for membership of the Lyke Wake Club. For many people the Lyke Wake Walk provides their only taste of long distance walking while for others it is the first step towards a new realm of walking with its own character, challenges and rich variety of rewards.

The Cleveland Way

THE Cleveland Way was opened in 1969. It was Britain's second official long distance path to be opened under the provisions of the 1949 National Parks and Access to Countryside Act, following on from the Pennine Way in 1965. Starting at Helmsley, the path travels three-quarters of the way round the perimeter of the National Park, taking in the Hambleton Hills, the Cleveland Hills and one of the finest stretches of Heritage Coast in the country between Staithes and Scarborough. The route then continues along the coast to Filey. Although one of the best defined and waymarked routes in the area it is also the most strenuous. Thorough planning and preparation are therefore strongly advised before undertaking the walk. The effort involved is undoubtedly worthwhile as no other long distance path captures such a rich variety of walking, scenery and history within such a short distance. In all respects the Cleveland Way makes a highly recommended walk.

Opposite: Route map of the **Cleveland Way**.

(Tony Wimbush)

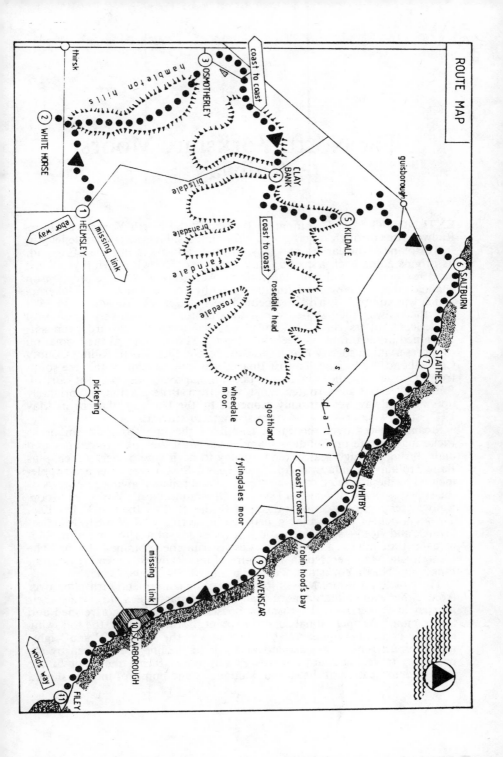

The North Yorkshire Moors Railway

EXTENDING from Grosmont to Pickering, the North Yorkshire Moors Railway runs through superb scenery for almost all its entire 18 mile length. It is also one of the earliest and most historic railways in northern England, its origins going back a century and a half to 1832 when Whitby felt the need for better inland communications. Accordingly, George Stephenson engineered a horse-worked line between the coastal town and Pickering which was completed in 1836. Locomotive haulage was introduced in 1847 and the railway then settled down to a century of relatively uneventful existence until its rural tranquility was shattered by closure proposals contained in the infamous Beeching Report. The upshot was the formation of a preservation society which, assisted by the then North Riding County Council and the English Tourist Board, was able to acquire the line south from Grosmont, the remaining portion surviving as part of British Railways' Esk Valley route. What was then Britain's longest privately operated railway was formally reopened by the Duchess of Kent in May 1973, since when it has gone from strength to strength.

Steam services over the entire length of the line from Grosmont to Pickering operate on Sundays from Easter until the end of October and daily during the high season (end of May to beginning of September, plus Bank Holiday Mondays in April and May). Steam workings are supplemented by diesel-hauled trains or 'scenic diesel railcars' giving fine views of the superb scenery of Newton Dale. At Grosmont, North Yorkshire Moors Railway services connect with those of British Rail on the Esk Valley line. Through tickets are available between Pickering and Whitby/Middlesbrough and vice versa. All the above services are subject to alteration. Up-to-date time-tables and further details can be obtained from: The Commercial Manager, North Yorkshire Moors Railway, Pickering Station, Pickering, North Yorkshire. Tel: Pickering (0751) 72508/73535.

The North Yorkshire Moors Railway can be conveniently travelled over from either end. Slightly more than half the passengers now start their journey at Pickering, but Grosmont boasts the main locomotive shed and thus remains the operational departure point. For this reason, the following route description commences at Grosmont and the terms 'left' and 'right' relate respectively to the east and west side of the line (i.e. as seen by the passenger travelling south towards Pickering and facing the front of the train). Identification of the various landmarks and points of interest should

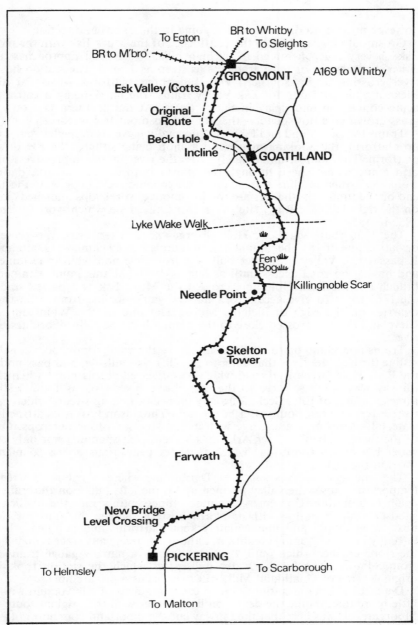

To Egton
BR to Whitby
To Sleights
BR to M'bro'.
GROSMONT
A169 to Whitby
Esk Valley (Cotts.)
Original Route
Beck Hole
Incline
GOATHLAND
Lyke Wake Walk
Fen Bog
Killingnoble Scar
Needle Point
Skelton Tower
Farwath
New Bridge Level Crossing
PICKERING
To Helmsley
To Scarborough
To Malton

(There are also stations at Levisham and Newtondale Halt)

however present no difficulty when going in the opposite direction.

Grosmont village, close to the confluence of the Murk Esk with the river Esk, is very much hemmed in by high hills. Most road approaches are either very narrow or have gradients as steep as 1 in 3. The station has a level crossing at its southern end and three platforms—two for the Pickering line and one for Esk Valley trains, the latter being a cause of acute congestion and delay in busier times. At the northern end only a grass-grown area now denotes the site of Grosmont Ironworks.

Trains for Goathland and Pickering normally leave from the left-hand or up platform, the booking office and a shop being situated on the down platform. They almost immediately cross the river by the impressive stone bridge and gather speed through the tunnel, both these structures dating from 1847 when the line was adapted for locomotive haulage. At the far end of the tunnel on the left are the locomotive workshops and sheds and on the right is Lease Rigg, site of an ironstone mine which worked from 1862 to 1874.

The 1836 route via Beck Hole diverges soon afterwards, the present deviation line of 1865 beginning its continuous 1 in 49 climb to Goathland. It passes Esk Valley, a hamlet built for ironstone and whinstone miners and having no road access until as late as 1951. At this point a mineral branch left the Beck Hole line, crossed the Murk Esk and passed under the 1865 route to give access to a narrow gauge incline from whinstone quarries on the edge of Sleights Moor. The line of the Whinstone or Cleveland Dyke is crossed close to the point where the railway bridges the river.

Trains now climb on to a ledge high above the valley floor, occasionally visible through the trees that cling to the cliff-like hillside, and pass under the Beck Hole-Green End road which was diverted at this point when the railway was built. A curve to the east above Beck Hole is followed by three crossings of Eller Beck, a usually innocent-looking stream which can rise six feet in a few hours after heavy rain. Thomason Foss is an attractive waterfall in this dramatic gorge with its massive sandstone outcrops. One of the three bridges—Water Ark—has a skew arch spanning not only the water but also a footbridge which provides pedestrians access to picnic spots in the glades beyond.

The line again curves south at Darnholm, where a tributary stream temporarily causes the valley to open up on the left, but soon the train is again in a cutting. One emerges almost imperceptibly into the idyllically sited Goathland station with its North Eastern signals, diminutive signal box, water cranes and immaculately kept platforms and buildings. It is virtually in pre-Grouping condition, although scarcely any trace remains of the stone crusher which until 1948 was fed by a narrow gauge tramway from Silhowe. The former water mill, after which the station took its original name of Goathland Mill, still survives as a private house.

Departure from the station is on an easier gradient of 1 in 90, and within little more than a mile the deviation line merges with the original route at Moorgates. It was here that the railway cut the moorland common in two, putting an end to the days when it was possible to travel from the coast to the western edge of the Cleveland Hills without encountering a single wall or fence. To facilitate the movement of stock an attractive stone archway known as the Cattle Arch was built under the line at this point, and a gatehouse erected in which a railwayman lived rent free in order to perform his duties. Both these structures survive and can clearly be seen on the right-hand side of the line.

The summit of the line, close to the 550 feet contour at Ellerbeck, precedes the entrance to the unique Newtondale. Once described as 'in many ways the finest example of glacial-lake overflow in England,' it is certainly among the most impressive of Yorkshire's Ice Age relics, being formed from the overspill from a huge lake eleven miles long and about 400 feet deep in Eskdale. Bracken, heather and the subtle colouring of the encircling moors combine to form an unforgettable scene. The line twists and turns, passing on the left Fen Bog which is now a forty acre nature reserve managed by the Yorkshire Naturalists' Trust. In another two miles is Needle Point (right), the needle being a natural arch in the side of the sandstone cliff where hawks once bred. The striking crags on the opposite side of the line include Yew Tree Scar, formed from Kellaways Rock—so named after the village in southern England—which glows a rich yellow in the afternoon sun.

Just beyond Yew Tree Scar is Newtondale Halt, opened in 1981 especially for passengers wishing to explore the valley on foot. Waymarked walks lead to Rapers Farm, Needle Point and Levisham station (see section on the Forests of the North York Moors). The halt has no road access, so it is important to study the timetable in order to avoid being marooned! Two

GROSMONT STATION

65

miles south is the site of Newtondale Ironworks where a shaft was sunk between 1857 and 1867 to extract ironstone from the cornbrash beds; it proved abortive, but traces of the railway siding can still be seen. Above is the prominent landmark of Skelton Tower, built as a castellated folly by the Rev. Robert Skelton of Levisham about 1850.

This stretch of line runs through considerable afforestation, particularly on the right-hand side where the trees have helped deer and pine marten to become re-established. On the right, ¾-mile beyond Skelton Tower, is The Grange, now a field activity centre but formerly the Raindale Inn where horses were changed during the early days of operation. Two features of which only remnants remain are Raindale Siding and Raindale Mill—an ancient building with a wooden overshot waterwheel which milled corn up to 1918, and more recently was moved stone by stone to form a working exhibit at York Castle Museum.

Next comes Levisham station, a place possessing almost magical qualities in its apparent remoteness from all habitation. Yet less than half a mile away on the plateau above the west side of the valley is Newton-upon-Rawcliffe, until recently accessible from the dale floor only by a narrow zig-zag path. An amusing anecdote in Oswald Harland's **Yorkshire North Riding** relates how the author arrived at the station in 1920 with a huge trunk, and thought he had indeed come to the end of the world when told that his destination of Newton could only be gained by a treacherous climb of 350 feet. He eventually paid the stationmaster's two boys five shillings to lug the trunk up the path. Levisham village is 1½ miles away on the east side of the line and again can only be reached by a climb of 300 feet.

The next few miles of the line run through extensive conifer plantations which have largely replaced the traditional hardwoods, although there are pockets of ash, birch and hazel as well as patches of rush and moss fed by springs from the valley sides. Two miles of virtually straight track lead to Farwarth (or Farworth), where one of a pair of early lineside cottages is now used as a field activity centre. Sidings once trailed into a small quarry, while on the opposite hillside can be seen the medieval dyke forming part of Blansby hunting park. The line again pursues a sinuous course until Newton Dale suddenly broadens into the Vale of Pickering at New Bridge. Here a two-foot gauge tramway formerly extended for two miles through Gundale Woods to quarries near Cawthorn. The signal box alongside the skew level crossing now controls the whole of the Pickering end of the line by means of remotely-controlled colour-light signals and power-operated points.

Within a matter of minutes the train now passes Pickering Trout Farm and runs at the foot of the castle to enter the terminus. It is the end of a journey through a superb stretch of countryside which is undoubtedly seen at its best by rail. The station, now forming the administrative headquarters of the railway, has suffered visually from the loss of its distinctive overall roof in 1951, but the quality of the stonework —and the large shop within the buildings—provide some compensation.

Reference
Section

General Information

NORTH YORK MOORS NATIONAL PARK

The North York Moors National Park was created in November 1952—the sixth in England and Wales. It includes some of the finest moorland and coastal scenery in Britain. One of the features of the moorlands is the way the road follows the ridges, giving fine views into the dales. The Blakey Ridge road between Castleton and Hutton-le-Hole reaches a height of 1,380 feet above sea level. A most useful companion is the Ordnance Survey Tourist Map of the area. **Please drive carefully on the unfenced moorland roads and give the sheep right of way.**

WALKING ON THE NORTH YORK MOORS

There are over 1,100 miles of public rights-of-way in the North York Moors National Park. The routes are marked on the one-inch to the mile Ordnance Survey Tourist Map and on the 1:50,000 maps (sheets 93, 94, 100, 101). In addition, many are clearly waymarked and signposted—great care should be taken to follow the correct route. Walkers can use any of the Forestry Commission roads in the area but must not light fires or pick plants. The Commission issues a map showing all facilities.

Guided walks of between two and eight miles suitable for all the family are arranged by the

National Park during the season. They start from several locations—consult the current 'Events' leaflet published by the Park for full details. Other National Park leaflets cover moorland safety and long-distance walks—i.e. the Cleveland Way and the Lyke Wake Walk. A series of leaflets entitled 'Waymark' describe short family walks.

Examples of walks specially recommended are:- Helmsley to Rievaulx (3½ miles); Sutton Bank to the White Horse of Kilburn (allow about 2 hours); Ellerburn (3 mile circular walk from Thornton Dale); Farndale 'daffodil walk' from Low Mill to Church Houses (allow 2 hours for the return journey); Forge Valley (many fine paths by riverside and through woodland); Mallyan Spout from Goathland; Beggars Bridge from Egton Bridge (allow one hour).

FOR FURTHER INFORMATION

Visit the Danby Lodge National Park Centre in the Esk Valley. It offers visitors an interpretive exhibition, illustrated talks, films and refreshments, and operates a local Tourist Information Service. Open daily April to September, 10.0 a.m. - 6.0 p.m. (also daily in October and at weekends in February, March and November, 10.0 a.m. - 5.0 p.m. The grounds extend to 13 acres including formal gardens, woodland and riverside meadow.

Sutton Bank Information Centre provides an exhibition area, information desk, bookshop and a light refreshment bar. It is open daily, Easter to end of October, 11.0 a.m. - 5.0 p.m. Pickering Station Information Centre features displays on the early history of the North Yorkshire Moors Railway and the scenery of Newtondale.

Details can also be obtained by writing to the Information Service, North York Moors National Park, The Old Vicarage, Bondgate, Helmsley. The local offices of the Forestry Commission are at 42 Eastgate, Pickering (all Commission guides are available from here, postage extra). Accommodation lists are available from Hambleton District Council, Council Offices, The Old Vicarage, Northallerton; and Ryedale District Council, Ryedale House, Malton.

Two National Trust properties on the edge of the North York Moors ...

RIEVAULX TERRACE & TEMPLES 2¼ m NW of Helmsley on B1257

Beautiful half-mile long terrace terminating at each end and with a classical eighteenth century temple.

OPEN: April to end October: every day (except Good Friday), 10.30 - 6.00

ADMISSION: Friday to Monday, 90p; Tuesday to Thursday, 80p.

NUNNINGTON HALL (4½m SE of Helmsley, 1½m N of B1257)

Large 16th and 17th century manor house on the bank of the River Rye. Home of the Carlisle Collection of miniature rooms. Teas served in the Dining Room.

OPEN: April to end October: Tuesday, Wednesday, Thursday, Saturday and Sunday, 2.0 - 6.0. Bank Holiday Monday, 11.0 - 6.0.

ADMISSION: £1

National Trust members are admitted **FREE**

Helmsley and the Hambletons

HELMSLEY
Black Swan Hotel; Crown Hotel; Feathers Hotel; Feversham Arms Hotel; Royal Oak. Licensed restaurants. Banks. Numerous shops including cafes, gift shops, fish and chip shop and garages. Market day Friday. Toilets. Youth hostel. Bus services to Pickering, Scarborough, Stokesley and Thirsk.

PLACES TO VISIT
Helmsley Castle: Path to the castle is opposite the church. Outer defences consist of two ditches separated by a steep sided earthwork. The remaining part of the keep gives some indication of the castle's size. Opening hours as Byland Abbey (see below).
Duncombe Park, Helmsley: The magnificent parkland contains formal gardens and two 18th century temples, situated on a terrace similar to that at Rievaulx (see below). Wednesdays, May to August, 10.0 a.m. - 4.0 p.m.
Roppa Edge: Can be reached by a two-mile path from Newgate Bank on the Helmsley - Stokesley road or by car along the four mile gated road which begins near Helmsley church. Famous—or perhaps infamous—for its controversial aluminium sculptures commissioned by the Yorkshire Arts Association from Austin Wright.
Rievaulx Abbey: The earliest Cistercian abbey in Yorkshire, it has not suffered as much damage by the weather and the hands of man as many similar buildings. The picturesque ruins lie in the narrow valley of the river Rye a few miles north of Helmsley. Car park and toilets for visitors. Opening hours as Byland Abbey (see below).
Rievaulx Terrace: Wide grass terrace, providing excellent views of the abbey below and having a temple at either end. National Trust property. Entrance signposted from Helmsley - Stokesley road (Open daily, beginning of April to end of October, 10.30 a.m. - 6.0 p.m.)
Sutton Bank: The top of the steep 1 in 4 hill presents a superb view over the Vale of York to the Pennines. An indicator at the south side of the road points out the various places of interest. Nearby, to the right, is Lake Gormire. Enjoy a walk along the escarpment edge to the gliding station. There are large car parks at the top of the bank.
Kilburn White Horse: A huge turf-cut figure on the hillside near the village of Kilburn. Executed in 1857, it measures 312 ft by 228 ft and is unique in the north of England. There is a car park at the foot of the horse by the side of the steep White Horse Bank. Alternatively, it can be reached on foot from Sutton Bank by following the 1½ mile waymarked White Horse Walk.
Robert Thompson's, Kilburn: Here one can visit the workshops and showrooms of 'The Mouseman', the name by which Robert Thompson affectionately came to be called. His trade mark was a carved mouse and it appeared on all his furniture which today can be seen throughout the country. The tradition has continued under the direction of his grandsons.

FREEDOM OF RYEDALE HOLIDAYS

SPECIALISTS IN HOLIDAYS IN NORTH YORKSHIRE

HOLIDAY COTTAGES. Cottages, farmhouses and other interesting properties situated in the spectacular countryside of the North York Moors and surrounding areas. Available all year and for weekends.

Colour brochure available.

FARMHOUSE HOLIDAYS. Spend a week on a farm in the National Park enjoying the full and traditional Yorkshire hospitality.

Brochure available.

ACTIVITY & INTEREST HOLIDAYS. A wide selection of holidays ranging from a guided 'Yorkshire Explorer' to Cycling, Riding, Spinning, Walking, Coast Discovery, Children's unaccompanied and many more. Accommodation in farmhouses, hotels, activity centres or youth hostels.

Colour brochure available.

CYCLE HIRE. Take in the country air and enjoy the beauty of the area by bicycle. We have a fleet of fully equipped touring cycles and tandems available for hire by the ½, full day, or week.

CHAUFFEUR DRIVEN CAR TOURS. Let us show you the best parts of the area in the comfort of a large chauffeur driven car. 2 hour, half or full day tours available.

PONY TREKKING & RIDING. Full, half day or evening treks available all year which take in some of the most spectacular country. Also riding lessons and inŝtruction.

TOURIST INFORMATION. Our Tourist Information Centre holds comprehensive stocks of guides, maps, publications and information on the Moors and local area. We are able to help with any visitors enquiries and can arrange or issue: Moorsrail Tickets, Fishing Licences, United Bus Co. 'Explorer' tickets, and tickets for local events.

We also offer a full Accommodation Booking Service for hotels, guesthouses, B & B, self catering, and Youth Hostels.

For information on any of the above please contact the address below:

Freedom of Ryedale Holidays, Dept. DNY.,
23a Market Place, Helmsley, N. Yorks.
Tel. Helmsley (0439) 70775. 24hr answer service.

Tourist Information

The showrooms are housed in a picturesque half-timbered Elizabethan house.

Coxwold: Shandy Hall: Home of Laurence Sterne, the great humorist, who was the local vicar from 1760 until his death in 1768. Now houses a collection of items related to Sterne and his writings. Wednesdays, early June to end of September, 2.0 p.m. - 5.0 p.m.

Newburgh Priory: A 12th century Augustinian priory with later alterations and additions. Has associations with Oliver Cromwell. Wild water garden and collection of rock plants; also walled garden. ¾-mile south of Coxwold. Wednesdays, beginning of July to end of August, 2.0 p.m. - 5.0 p.m.

Byland Abbey: Once the largest Cistercian church in England, the abbey is today noted for the remains of its great circular window and its glazed tiles. Situated on the minor road linking Coxwold with Ampleforth. Daily, 9.30 a.m. - 7.0 p.m. (5.30 p.m. in October, March and April; 4.0 p.m. November to February).

Gilling Castle: Original Norman keep with 16th and 18th century additions. On the B1363 Helmsley - York road. Daily (except Sundays) 10.0 a.m. - 12.0 noon, 2.0 p.m. - 4.0 p.m.

Nunnington Hall: Just off B1257 Helmsley - Malton road north of Hovingham. 16th century manor house with panelled hall and staircase. National Trust property. April to October, Tuesdays to Sundays (except Fridays) 2.0 p.m. - 6.0 p.m.

NATURE TRAIL

Sutton Bank Nature Trail: Starts on the northern side of the road at the top of Sutton Bank. Gives fine views of Lake Gormire and Whitestone Cliff.

INFORMATION CENTRE

Sutton Bank Information Centre (for further details see 'General Information').

YOUTH HOSTEL

Helmsley.

CARAVAN SITES

Foxholme Touring Caravan Park, Harome. Tel. Helmsley 70416. Touring caravans, motor caravans. Open April to October.

Low Cleaves, Sutton under Whitestone Cliff, Thirsk. Tel. Sutton 229. Touring caravans, motor caravans, tents. Open May to September.

FISHING

River Rye—Hawnby: Hawnby Hotel, Tel. Bilsdale 202. Day tickets and weekly tickets.

River Rye—Nunnington: Estate Office, Nunnington. Tel. Nunnington 202. Day tickets.

Lake Arden: Mr Mott, Keepers Cottage, Arden Hall. Tel. Bilsdale 343. Day tickets, boat for hire.

Elm Hag Lake: Oldstead, near Coxwold. Mr P. Bradley, Oldstead. Tel. Coxwold 223. Day tickets.

RIDING

Mr A. C. Barker, The Riding School, Helmsley. Tel. Helmsley 70355.

A. W. & S. J. Cain, Shaken Bridge Farm, Hawnby. Tel. Bilsdale 225 or 252.

Mr R. Tate, Hesketh Grange, Boltby, Thirsk. Tel. Thirsk 537375.

THE BLACK SWAN
Oldstead, Coxwold, York

Mine Hosts: Donnie & Jackie MacArthur
Telephone Coxwold (034 76) 387

In perhaps one of the most beautiful stretches of National Park in North Yorkshire, deep in the heart of James Herriott country, Oldstead in Ryedale nestles into a South-facing slope of the Hambleton Hills, and is surrounded by truly magnificent walks throughout the adjacent Forest of Ampleforth. It is situated mid-way between the famous White Horse of Kilburn and the splendidly peaceful 12th Century ruins of Byland Abbey, and is an ideal touring base from which to explore the treasures of the North Yorkshire National Park.

The Black Swan, with its bow-windowed stone exterior, overlooks rolling meadow and woodland and presents a pleasing picture. Built in the 18th Century, on one of the main drover's routes from the North Yorkshire Moors, to the Vale of York, many improvements have been made over the years. Visitors will, however, be pleased to see all the characteristics of a country tavern have been retained.

Bar snacks and basket meals are available throughout the Spring and Summer months, lunchtime and from 7 p.m. onwards. An enviable reputation is enjoyed for Evening Grills, Basket Meals and a wide selection of the finest quality Steaks at exceptional value. Speciality of the house: Home-made Steak and Kidney Pie, Quiche and mouth-watering Pizzas. Evening meals are provided throughout the year. A la carte meals and selective wine list can be enjoyed subject to notice.

A modern accommodation wing has been added to the rear of the Inn, with each unit having its own shower, toilet, central heating, etc.

A warm welcome is extended to all who visit this friendly Inn from Donnie and Jackie and it is a must for those either travelling through the area, or visiting the Workshop of that great craftsman in English Oak, Robert (The Mouseman) Thompson, at nearby Kilburn. Eight miles from Helmsley, Thirsk and Easingwold.

Free House

Kirkbymoorside and the Southern Dales

THE MAIN CENTRES
Kirkbymoorside: Black Swan; George and Dragon Hotel; King's Head Hotel; White Horse Hotel; White Swan. There are numerous shops and banks, a chemist, fish and chip shop, garages, cafe, toilets. Market day, Wednesday. Bus service to Pickering and Helmsley.
Hutton-le-Hole: The Crown Inn. Post office, store, craft centres, gift shops, tea shop, filling station, toilets. Ryedale Folk Museum (see below).

PLACES TO VISIT:
Kirkdale Minster: Just off the main A170 Helmsley - Pickering road west of Kirkbymoor-side. A tiny Saxon church famous for its Saxon sundial (c. 1055). A place not to be missed.
Hutton-le-Hole: Ryedale Folk Museum: Contains a fine range of local antiques, craftsmen's tools and farm and household implements. There are a number of reconstructed buildings at the rear, including a 16th century manor house, a cruck cottage, an Elizabethan glass furnace and a smithy. Daily, Easter to October, 2.0 p.m. - 6.0 p.m. (July and August, 11.0 a.m. - 7.0 p.m.).
Lastingham church: This village at the foot of the North York Moors between Hutton-le-Hole and Pickering had a religious settlement as early as 654A.D. The superb Norman crypt of

the present church dates from c. 1078 and is reached down a flight of steps.

INFORMATION CENTRE
Ryedale Folk Museum, Hutton-le-Hole (see above). Tel. Lastingham 367.

CARAVAN SITES
Wren's of Ryedale Caravan Site, Gale Lane, Nawton. Tel. Helmsley 71260. Touring caravans, motor caravans, tents. Open April to mid-October.

Forestry Commission, Spiers House, Cropton, Pickering. Touring caravans, motor caravans, tents. Open Easter to October.

Blacksmith's Arms Hotel, Hartoft End, Rosedale Abbey, Pickering. Tel. Lastingham 331. Touring caravans. Open all year.

Rosedale Caravan & Camping Parks, Rosedale Abbey, Pickering. Tel. Lastingham 272. Touring caravans, motor caravans, tents. Open March to October.

RIDING

Messrs. D. & N. Grice, Mount Pleasant, High Lane, Nawton. Tel. Helmsley 71672.
Mr. W.D.C. Needham, Medd's Farm, Rosedale, Pickering. Tel. Lastingham 358.
Miss H.A. Hebron, Red House Riding Stables, Rosedale Head, Pickering. Tel. Lastingham 203.

Pickering and the South-East

THE MAIN CENTRES

Pickering: There is a good selection of hotels and inns in Pickering. There are also numerous shops, banks, garages and cafes. Toilets, tourist information centre. Market day. Monday. Bus service to Whitby, Scarborough, Helmsley and Malton. Rail service to Grosmont.

Thornton Dale: Buck Hotel; Hall Hotel; New Inn. There are numerous shops, artist's studio, licensed restaurant, fish and chip shop, cafes and a garage, toilets. Bus service to Pickering, Scarborough, Whitby, Helmsley and Malton.

PLACES TO VISIT

North Yorkshire Moors Railway: One of the longest privately operated railways in the country, extending from Pickering to Grosmont and running through the scenically superb Newtondale. Other stations are at Goathland and Levisham. A regular steam and diesel service operates throughout the season. Full details from the North Yorkshire Moors Railway at Pickering Station.

Pickering Castle: A 12th century structure on a Norman mound. Compact and attractive, it offers plesant views to the west. Opening hours as Byland Abbey.

Pickering: Beck Isle Museum of Rural Life: A fine Regency building situated at the side of Pickering Beck. Contains a large number of exhibits of local history and folk life. Daily, Easter to mid-October, 10.30 a.m. - 12.30 p.m., 2.0 p.m. - 5.30 p.m. (10.30 a.m. - 7.0 p.m. in August).

Hole of Horcum: A spectacular natural hollow to the west of the A169 Whitby road north of Pickering. Best seen from the top of Saltersgate Bank where there is a car park. A popular centre for hang gliding.

Low Dalby: Forest Visitor Centre: Interpretive centre covering many aspects of forestry work and containing a display of stuffed birds and animals likely to be seen in the forests. Open April to end of October.

Ebberston Hall: Small but attractive country house built in 1718. On the main A170 Pickering Scarborough road east of Thornton Dale.

Daily, Easter to mid-September, 2.0 p.m. - 6.0 p.m.

FOREST DRIVES, WALKS AND TRAILS

Bridestones Moor Nature Walk: Starts at the Bridestones car park on the Dalby Forest Drive (see below). A ten minute walk leads to the large weathered rock outcrops on the moor.

Dalby Forest Drive: Toll road through the forest linking Low Dalby with Hackness. There are a number of car parks and picnic sites en route.

Newtondale Forest Walks: Three walks based on Newtondale Halt on the North Yorkshire Moors Railway. Distances vary from 2¼ to 7 miles. Show many trees, plants and flowers as well as various aspects of Forestry Commission work.

Sneverdale Forest Trail: Just outside the village of Low Dalby on the Dalby Forest Drive. 1 or 3 miles.

INFORMATION CENTRES

Pickering Station Information Centre. Tel. Pickering 73791. For further details see under 'General Information'.

Forest Visitor Centre, Low Dalby, Pickering. Tel. Pickering 60295.

YOUTH HOSTEL

Lockton, near Pickering.

CARAVAN SITES

Upper Carr Caravan Site, Lane View, Black Bull, Pickering. Tel. Pickering 73115. Touring caravans, motor caravans, tents. Open March to October.

Black Bull Inn Caravan Site, Malton Road, Pickering. Tel. Pickering 72528. Touring caravans, motor caravans, tents. Open March to October.

Wayside Caravan Park, Cliff Road, Wrelton, Pickering. Tel. Pickering 72608. Touring caravans, motor caravans, tents. Open Easter to October.

Overbrook, Thornton Dale. Tel. Thornton Dale 417. Touring caravans, motor caravans. Open Easter to October.

Jasmine Caravan Park, Snainton, Scarbor-

NEWBRIDGE ROAD, PICKERING
Just past the Railway Station
Telephone 0751-73101

Come, See & Feed the Fish

Leaflet, sticker & bag of food - 25p each

Fresh Trout for Sale
any quantity

95p per lb.
5 lb. pack £4.75
cleaned ready to freeze

Oak Smoked Trout
£1.60 per lb.

Open 7 days a week
9 a.m. - 5 p.m.

FISHING

It is hoped to have a 'Catch your own' fishing lake open by Spring Bank holiday, next to the Railway station car park.

Rod, bait hooks hire, plus 1st 1lb. of Trout-£2.50 each
Own tackle plus 1st 1lb. of Trout-£2.00 each
All Trout caught must be bought.

Lake stocked daily

ough 85240. Touring caravans, motor caravans, tents. Open April to October.
St. Helen's-in-the-Park Caravan Site, Wykeham, Scarborough. Tel. Scarborough 862771. Open March to October.

FISHING
Dalby Beck: Forestry Commission Information Centre, Low Dalby. Day tickets.
River Derwent (Hackness): Hackness Grange Hotel. Tel. Scarborough 69966. Day tickets. No Sunday fishing.

RIDING
Mrs R. Cook, Beck Isle Ponies, Wells Walk, Pickering. Tel. Pickering 72982.
Mr E. Garbutt, North Barker Stakes Farm, Lendale Lane, Pickering. Tel. Pickering 73730.
Mr G. Morley, The Hall Stables, Thornton Dale. Tel. Pickering 74297.
Snainton Riding Centre, Snainton, Scarborough. Tel. Scarborough 85218.
A.L. Dickinson, Heights Pony Trekking Centre, Sawdon Heights, Sawdon, Scarborough. Tel. Scarborough 85321.

Dalesman Books on the North York Moors

Area Guides

Explore Yorkshire by Car—The North York Moors
Exploring Captain Cook Country
Exploring the North York Moors
North York Moors A to Z
North Yorkshire Moors Railway (pictorial album)
Pickering (A Visitor's Guide)
Steam on the North York Moors
Thornton-le-Dale (A Visitor's Guide)
Ways of a Yorkshire Dale (Eskdale)
Whitby (A Visitor's Guide)

Books for the Walker

The Bilsdale Circuit
Cleveland Way
Crosses Walk
Long Distance Walks—The North York Moors
Lyke Wake Walk
Lyke Wake Lamentations
Walking on the North York Moors
Walks from Your Car
    1.   Bilsdale and the Hambletons
    2.   Eskdale and the Cleveland Coast
    3.   Rosedale and Farndale
White Rose Walk

Send S.A.E. for list of over 300 titles to:
DALESMAN PUBLISHING COMPANY LTD.,
CLAPHAM, Via LANCASTER, LA2 8EB.

The Esk Valley

THE MAIN CENTRES

Castleton: Downe Arms; Moorlands Hotel; The Eskdale Inn; The Robin Hood and Little John. Post Office, general stores, grocers, garage, National Westminster Bank, craft shop, Angling: Permits from post office. Toilets. Rail service to Whitby and Middlesbrough. Bus service to Guisborough and Danby.

Goathland: Goathland Hotel; Goathland Hydro; Mallyan Spout Hotel; Birch Hall Inn (Beck Hole). Post Office, stores, cafe, art gallery/craft shop. Bus service to Whitby and Pickering. Rail services to Pickering and Grosmont. Toilets, youth hostel at Wheeldale Lodge (1 mile).

Grosmont: Station Tavern. Post Office, general stores, cafe, toilets. Rail services to Whitby, Middlesbrough and Pickering.

Sleights: The Salmon Leap; The Plough. Post offices, stores, butchers, antique shops, cafe with boats for hire, fishing, putting green. Toilets, art gallery. Bus service to Pickering and Whitby. Rail service to Whitby and Middlesbrough.

PLACES TO VISIT

Danby Lodge National Park Centre: In the Esk Valley ½-mile east of Danby village and a one-mile walk from Danby railway station. A former shooting-lodge which has been adapted as a visitor centre for the North York Moors National Park. Fuller details are given under 'General Information'.

Mallyan Spout: A 70 ft high waterfall reached by following a path from the side of the Mallyan Spout Hotel at Goathland.

Roman road, Wheeldale Moor: One of the best preserved stretches of Roman road in the country. Reached by a short walk from Hunt House near Goathland or by road from Egton Bridge.

HISTORICAL TRAIL

Grosmont Historical Railway Trail: 3½ mile walk along the track bed of George Stephenson's original railway between Grosmont and Goathland via Beck Hole.

INFORMATION CENTRE

Danby Lodge National Park Centre (see General Information).

YOUTH HOSTELS

Westerdale, near Castleton.
Wheeldale, near Goathland.

FISHING

River Esk (Danby): April 1st to end of September. No Sunday fishing. Limited number of weekly tickets from Duke of Wellington Inn, Danby; Castleton Post Office; Danby Post Office; Hon. Sec., Danby & District Angling Club, 11 Dale End, Danby. Tel. Castleton 385. **Lockwood Beck Reservoir:** Alongside Whitby-Guisborough road. Northumbrian Water Authority licence required. Day tickets; boats available for hire. Contact Fishing Lodge, Lockwood Beck.

Scaling Dam Reservoir: Alongside Whitby-Guisborough road. Brown and rainbow trout. Day tickets available. Contact Fishing Lodge, Scaling Dam.

RIDING

D. L. Roberts, Sleights Riding School, Partridge Nest Farm, Eskdaleside, Sleights, Whitby. Tel. Whitby 810450.

Summerfield Riding and Trekking Centre, Church Farm, Aislaby, Whitby. Tel. Whitby 810086.

Cleveland Hills and Plain

THE MAIN CENTRES

Guisborough: There are a number of hotels, shops, banks, garages and cafes. Swimming pool, information centre. Bus service to Middlesbrough, Staithes, Whitby, Danby, Great Ayton, Stokesley and Redcar.

Great Ayton: Buck Hotel; Royal Oak Hotel; Tilesheds Inn. There are numerous shops including cafes and a fish and chip shop. Garages and filling station. Bus services to Stokesley, Guisborough, Middlesbrough.

Osmotherley: Golden Lion Hotel; Queen Catherine Hotel; Three Tuns Inn. Post office/general store, grocers, antique shop, Midland Bank, garage, cafe, fish and chip shop, craft shop, caravan site, toilets. Bus service to Stokesley and Northallerton.

PLACES TO VISIT

Guisborough Priory: An Augustinian foundation established in 1119 by Robert de Brus. The finest part of the priory left standing is the magnificent east end almost 100 feet high. Daily 9.30 a.m.-7.0 p.m. (5.30 p.m. in October, March and April; 4.0 p.m. November to February).

Roseberry Topping: Cleveland's Matterhorn, looking much higher than its actual 1,051 ft.

Easiest climb is from Newton-under-Roseberry by a track which begins at the southern end of the village. View from the summit includes much of Teesside and the surrounding moors.

Great Ayton: Captain Cook Museum: Originally the schoolroom where the young James Cook began his education. Reached up an external staircase. Open all year except Christmas week.

Hasty Bank: The summit of the B1257 Helmsley -Stokesley road. Offers magnificent views over Cleveland and across to Roseberry Topping. There is a Forestry Commission car park and a snack bar. A path climbs to the summit of Hasty Bank itself, 1,304 ft above sea level.

Scarth Nick: A narrow pass between the hills on the road from Swainby to Osmotherley. At Sheepwash there are a number of car parks in a picturesque moorland setting with an opportunity for children to play in the stream.

Osmotherley: Lady Chapel: Built in the early 16th century. A half hour walk from Osmotherley. Open all year.

Mount Grace Priory: Just off the main A19 Thirsk - Teesside road a mile south of Osmotherley. The best preserved Carthusian monastery in Britain. One of the original 'cells' in which the monks lived has been restored to its former condition. Opening hours as Guisborough Priory.

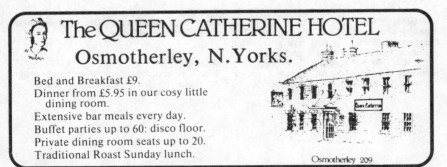

INFORMATION CENTRE
Guisborough: Chapel Beck Gallery and Tourist Information Centre. Open all year, Monday to Saturday, 10.0 a.m. - 5.30 p.m.

CARAVAN SITES
Tockett's Mill, Skelton Road, Guisborough. Tel. Guisborough 35161. Touring caravans, motor caravans, tents. Open April to end October.
Toft Hill Farm, Kirkby-in-Cleveland. Tel. Stokesley 712469. Touring caravans, motor caravans, tents. Open April to October.

Cote Ghyll Caravan Park, Osmotherley, Northallerton. Tel. Osmotherley 425. Touring caravans, motor caravans, tents. Open April to October.

FISHING
Cod Beck Reservoir: Day tickets from Osmotherley Post Office.

RIDING
Miss A. Nelson, Crossbank, Whorlton, Swainby, Northallerton. Tel. Hutton Rudby 700550.

Whitby and the Coast

THE MAIN CENTRES
Whitby: There is a good selection of hotels, shops, banks, garages and cafes. Toilets, swimming pool, golf course, youth hostel, Tourist Information centre, New Quay Road, Bus service to Pickering, Scarborough, Guisborough and Robin Hood's Bay. Rail service to Middlesbrough and Pickering.

Robin Hood's Bay: Bay Hotel. Dolphin Inn. Laurel Inn. Victoria Hotel. Grosvenor Hotel. Two post offices, stores, butchers, fish and chip shop, restaurant, cafes, gift shops, filling station, Barclays Bank, National Westminster Bank, Midland Bank. Toilets, youth hostel (1 mile). Bus service to Whitby.

Staithes: Captain Cook Inn. Cod and Lobster. Black Lion. Royal George Hotel. Post office, cafes, newsagent, gift shops, pottery/studio, art and photo gallery, grocers, butcher, fish and chip shop, garage, caravan site, toilets. Bus service to Guisborough and Whitby.

PLACES TO VISIT
Sandsend: Mulgrave Woods: Extensive woodland bordering two ravines and encompassing remains of 13th century castle. Daily (except Wednesdays, Saturdays and Sundays in May).
Whitby Abbey: Magnificent ruins in a commanding position overlooking the town. Shows work of the 12th to 15th centuries. Daily 9.30 a.m.-7.0 p.m. (5.30 p.m. October, March and April; 4.0 p.m. November to February).
Whitby: St. Mary's Church: Close to the abbey and best approached up the 199 steps from the harbour side. A fascinating structure containing an extraordinary mixture of style and design.

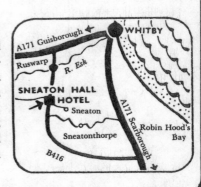

Whitby Museum: Includes shipping gallery with Captain Cook relics. May to September, weekdays 9.30 a.m. - 5.30 p.m., Sundays 2.0 p.m.-5.0 p.m. Also limited opening in winter months.

TRAILS
These include the **Falling Foss Forest Trail** (approached from the B1416 at Red Gates, south of Whitby); the nearby **May Beck Farm Trail; Ravenscar Geological Trail;** and **Silpho Forest Trail** (at Reasty Bank overlooking Harwood Dale).

INFORMATION CENTRES
Whitby Tourist Information Centre, New Quay Road, Whitby. Tel. 60274.
Ravenscar National Trust Shop and Information Centre. Open April to October, daily except Mondays. Tel. Scarborough 870138.

YOUTH HOSTELS
Boggle Hole, near Robin Hood's Bay (superior grade). Whitby.

CARAVAN SITES
Whitby Holiday Village, Saltwick Bay, Whitby. Tel. 602664. Touring caravans, motor caravans, tents. Open May to mid-September.
Northcliffe Caravan Park, High Hawsker, Whitby. Tel. Whitby 880567 and 880584. Touring caravans, motor caravans, tents. Open April to end of September.
York House, High Hawsker, Whitby. Tel. Whitby 880354. Touring caravans and motor caravans. Open March to October.

Grouse Hill Touring Caravan Park, Flask Bungalow Farm, Fylingdales, Whitby. Tel. Whitby 880543. Touring caravans, motor caravans, tents. Open April to October.
Rigg Farm Caravan Park, Stainsacre, Whitby. Tel. Whitby 880430. Touring caravans, motor caravans. Open March to October.
Burnt House Caravan Park, Ugthorpe, Whitby. Tel. Whitby 840291. Touring caravans, motor caravans. Open March to October.
Ugthorpe Lodge Caravan Park, Whitby. Tel. Whitby 840518. Touring caravans, motor caravans, tents. Open March to October.
Warp Mill Caravan Site, Staithes, Saltburn. Tel. Whitby 849291. Touring caravans, motor caravans. Open March to October.
Fern Farm, Hinderwell, Saltburn. Tel. Whitby 840350. Touring caravans, motor caravans, tents. Open March to October.

RIDING
R. T. Hearne, Low Moor House, Ugthorpe, Whitby. Tel. Whitby 840086.
Mr & Mrs G.J. Sadler, Fen Cottage, High Normanby, Robin Hood's Bay. Tel. Robin Hood's Bay 730.
L. & R. Turner, The Riding School, Whitby Road, Robin Hood's Bay.
Browside Trekking Centre, Ladysmith Farm, Ravenscar. Tel. Robin Hood's Bay 295.
Peakside Riding & Trekking Centre, Ravenscar. Tel. Scarborough 870423.
Pollard Riding School, Pollard Cottage, Ravenscar. Tel. Scarborough 870470.

The Old Hall Hotel

RUSWARP • WHITBY • YORKS. YO21 1NH

This most historic hotel in the Whitby area is a 17th century Jacobean Hall of elegant character and architectural interest, situated in its own grounds in Ruswarp village.

The hotel, tastefully furnished and decorated, retains the aura of leisurely tranquility and grandeur of former years which is apparent on entering the hall where wide stairs lead to a minstrel and picture gallery. There is a gracious "reading" lounge, separate TV lounge and an interesting "Settle" bar offering congeniality. The 20 bedrooms, each with differing character, some with shower or bath, all with hot and cold, are fitted with radio/baby listening system.

The relaxed informal atmosphere and comfortable accommodation, is enhanced by good food and the friendly hospitality of the resident proprietors. The mellowness and character of the hotel should captivate old and young alike, providing home from home comfort with that extra "something special".

The surrounding area offers unparallel opportunities for fishing, boating, sailing, walking, horseriding, golf, archaeological and geological exploration, or just quiet relaxation. The ancient fishing village of Whitby with its magnificent beach, safe bathing and varied holiday pastimes, is only a mile and a half away.

Close by are other fishing centres which offer striking comparisons to beautiful moorland villages, quiet picnic spots and the magnificent scenery of the 500 square miles of the North Yorkshire Moors National Park.

Licensed Restaurant serving optional a la carte evening meals.
Central heating. Car Park.
Spacious rear garden.
Reductions for children under 12 years.
Reductions for group bookings.
Reasonable tariff.
Open Easter to October; Christmas/New Year

Brochure and tariff from
John and Liz Rankin:
Telephone Whitby (0947) 602801

Mauley Cross